21st Century Handbook:
A Guide to Creating Health, Happiness
and Peace in a Stressful, Modern Day World

By Cynthia Blancaflor

Published by Platypus Publishing

Copyright © 2023 by Cynthia Blancaflor All Rights Reserved
ISBN 978-1-959555-61-2, Published by Platypus Publishing
Book Editing by Laura Esposito, Book Cover by Vianney Lopez

All rights reserved. No part of this book may be reproduced in any form by an electronic or mechanical means, including information storage and retrieval systems, without permission in writing from the author, except by a reviewer who may quote brief passages in a review.

Dedication:

For world peace and the healing of our planet, by starting with finding the peace within and healing ourselves. To my teachers who've shown me the way to healing, especially my best teachers, experience and intuition.

To my sister, mother, father and extended family who died from food-related illnesses. May future generations be more informed and empowered to choose to live longer, healthier, happier lives and learn of the ways in which the body can heal itself.

Table of Contents:

Introduction	1
Chapter 1: Know Thyself: Meditation as Medication	10
Chapter 2: Heal Thyself: Naturopathy, Food as Medicine	33
Chapter 3: Cannabis Cures: Our Misunderstood Cousin	56
Chapter 4: Entheogens (a.k.a. Psychedelics): Expanding the Gateway to Our Consciousness	68
Chapter 5: Gender and Sexuality: Loving the Spectrum of Who We Are and Who We Desire	93
Chapter 6: Love and Relationships: Self-Love, Intimacy and The Ways We Mate and Relate	111
Chapter 7: Communication: Relating, Involving, Resolving, Evolving	128
Chapter 8: Community: Being in Alignment, Finding Support, Being of Service in Our Purpose and Mentorship	144
Chapter 9: Financial Literacy: Money is Energy, Access and Experience	160
Chapter 10: Sustainability: Honoring Our Global Interconnectedness	176
References	201

Introduction:

As a Buddhist, I believe that we are all bodhisattvas or are sent here to relieve the suffering of others. This is why I wrote this book.

This book is for people who want change and are open to do the work to have a transformation. Or maybe you want to learn or get inspired to take better care of your health. Just know there is no magic pill. It's a series of actions, a lifestyle that will bring about a better quality of life with effort and consistency.

For many years, I've had conversations with people from all walks of life about the ways holistic practices like yoga, meditation, naturopathy, creative expression, community connection and nature time have helped me to create and maintain a state of wellness.

The joy you experience from the benefits of having a daily self-care routine is priceless. Caring for ourselves is a lifelong journey. I find the key is to be open to learning that there may be a better way than what we already know or have been taught, especially if we are currently unwell and unhappy.

My mother, her three sisters, my grandmother, and my eldest sister all died from type 2 diabetes or related complications. I later learned that type 2 diabetes is preventable, related to a high-sugar diet and inactivity.

I saw how they suffered, tied to pharmaceutical drugs, dialysis, needles and surgery. I watched as eating certain foods ultimately made them sick. Growing up, I did not have the knowledge, but an intuition that food and health were linked.

The psychology of food is so deeply rooted in our traditions and cultures that we may continue to eat foods that make us sick because that's what everyone else is doing. I was one of those people. Our bodies can grow accustomed to eating toxic foods and we can feel fine—until we don't.

I found myself dealing with severe digestive issues and taking Western medications to treat them and then getting sicker as a result. This sparked my desire to find other ways to heal myself. By listening more closely to my body, I was led to naturopathic remedies and teachers who helped me unlearn toxic habits and relearn how to heal myself naturally. It was liberating.

I was always intrigued by holistic medicine or naturopathy that uses natural cures that originated in the Eastern world thousands of years ago and uses natural foods and herbs as a form of preventative care.

What I saw modeled as "health care" growing up in the U.S. was conventional medicine that deals with symptoms of an illness, not the root cause. The allopathic approach used in the U.S. medical system goes back less than 300 years.

But Chinese and Tibetan medicine based on naturopathy have stood the test of time, with over 2,000 years of quality results.

When I was younger, my parents took multiple medications to "control" their diet-related conditions. One diabetic Auntie took steroids to control inflammatory issues like arthritis and dermatitis, but it also increases blood glucose which is dangerous for a diabetic. Another Auntie with diabetes had a complication during surgery and died.

My family endured six deaths caused by a disease we believed to have no cure. I knew there had to be a better way.

Being raised Filipino American, whenever I had a headache, my parents would say "take a Tylenol." And although it may have worked, it covered up a deeper issue. Later in life, I learned water makes up to 75% of the body. Proper hydration is key to wellness, and can determine how well a body fights illness. Now that I drink the necessary amount of water each day (about 3 liters or half of your body weight in ounces), I rarely have headaches.

When Western meds failed me, I found myself on the path to healing my chronic illnesses through naturopathic remedies. I found naturopathic teachers who recommended natural remedies that helped activate my body's own natural healing powers.

It makes sense to change the behaviors that cause the illness to heal the illness. That's why it's called preventative care. If you stay healthy by making healthy choices, then your illness goes away, or your chances of being sick are greatly reduced.

Prescribed drugs rank third as the leading cause of death in the US and Europe after heart disease and cancer. [Ref. 1] Western medicine is amazing if you are in an accident or have a medical emergency. But for chronic issues like diabetes, high blood pressure or depression, I believe that with better lifestyle choices and effective health tools, we can maintain overall wellness.

What's fascinating is that our physical health affects our mental health, which is why food is the starting point to wellness.

Just eat a meal rich in carbs, fat or processed foods then notice how sluggish you feel as opposed to when you eat whole foods like fruit, vegetables and grains that give you energy.

The human body alone produces over 109 chemicals to sustain us. What I've learned about preventative health care is that through proper hydration, a nutrient rich diet and many other self-care modalities, we can activate the body's ability to heal itself and feel more wellness and happiness in our lives.

My intention is to inspire self-empowerment and nurture the belief that we have the power to heal ourselves and feel well. I believe we are all healers. Why? Because no one is in your body but you, so listening to how things make you feel is key. Study yourself, there is a wealth of wisdom in your experience.

According to the World Health Organization, depression and anxiety went up 25% worldwide during the pandemic [Ref 7]. This was due to lockdown when many of us were forced to stay home in possibly toxic situations or we just slowed down with more time on our hands, causing us to face our own issues like never before.

It broke many of us down to our core. While some faced real crises like unemployment, illness and death, quarantine was traumatic for many of us. Some lucky people used this time to develop a new skill, explore a hobby, spend more time with loved ones and increase self-care routines.

Whatever state you were in, it was a chance to rebuild who we are. A new beginning. Now the world has opened back up, I see more people are inspired to choose a better quality of life and feel empowered to take action. I write this for you.

Choosing to be healthy starts with self-love. I've had stages in my life where not valuing myself led to illness and toxic situations. We all go through this, but the difference is whether we choose to learn from these lessons to become a better version of ourselves, or stay a victim of our suffering and unhealthy patterns.

Some people look at making lifestyle changes as drastic measures especially when "experts" are paid millions of dollars to debunk natural ways of healing. Just Google it and you can find an article saying that everything I share in this book is a lie.

The historic roots of why people believe in pharmaceuticals over natural cures in dealing with chronic illnesses started in the early 1900s which I will discuss in more detail later.

Sadly, the intention behind this miseducation was a multi-pronged approach by the oligarchs and plutocrats of the time to make money. Meanwhile they were making people sicker and dependent on the drugs. Sound familiar? Today there is a movement returning to the power of natural cures because they work. They did for me.

When someone with chronic illnesses takes several medications at a time just to "control" a disease and not ever cure it seems more extreme and dangerous to me.

We can help heal ourselves through the power of exercise, nutrition, hydration and even positive thinking.

How can we begin to transform our suffering to create more wellness in our lives? Mental health is the starting point. Finding that happiness from within is powerful and much more sustainable than any drug.

Choosing the path to heal ourselves ripples out to our relationships and then to our entire planet. I have seen this work in my own life when I have been a part of a healthy community, in a healthy partnership, living in a healthy environment in the San Francisco Bay area, California. We are all interconnected and affect each other.

This book's title, "21st Century Handbook: A Guide to Creating Health, Happiness and Peace in a Stressful, Modern Day World" speaks from a perspective of global citizenship based on the idea of global interconnectedness, or "the ability to function in an increasingly multicultural, international, yet interconnected environment. It fosters the development of individuals to become successful professionals, civic leaders, and informed citizens in a diverse national and global society" [Ref. 25].

The value system of accumulating profits over the well-being of the planet and future generations has caused the global threat of climate change along with many social challenges. The value system of sustainability which means meeting our own needs without compromising the ability of future generations to meet their own needs is what is needed now more than ever on every level of community, government and society. The wisdom of the Native American prophecy from the Cree tribe in Canada sums it up best, "When the last tree is cut, the last river poisoned, and the last fish dead, we will discover that we can't eat money." [Ref. 26]

Still don't believe we're all interconnected? COVID-19 virus first appeared in Wuhan, China in December 2019. By March 2020, the WHO, World Health Organization, declared COVID-19, a global pandemic. "Climate change is making outbreaks of disease more common and more dangerous. Over the past few decades, the number of emerging infectious diseases that spread to people — especially coronaviruses and other respiratory illnesses believed to have come from bats and birds — has skyrocketed." [Ref. 27] The time is ripe for us to wake up, see the truth of our inherent interconnectedness, think for ourselves beyond the herd and learn from the teachers and healers who are giving us the tools to create our best life right now.

7

It's time to look around with new eyes of reverence and appreciation. Every food, every product, every service and support system we rely on depends on the work of someone else. How different our world would be if we all behaved from this place of awareness.

What would change if we all accepted the truth of our global interconnectedness? Would world peace be more than a concept? What if we started with healing and valuing ourselves first versus judging what others are doing and telling them how to live their lives? Would we even have the time and interest to judge others if we were truly happy at home? Would we be more compassionate and kind to others if we truly felt well within our lives? Absolutely.

As I learn more and increase awareness and education about the best choices I can make for my health, happiness and wellness, I see the negative, unhappy behavior from others with more compassion now. Not everyone is happy, but it is a choice. My moods vary from time to time, but maintaining balance is key. I believe that if we know better, we do better.

When you are truly happy you exude positivity and peace. If you are not centered and grounded in your own power, perhaps consumed more with what others think of you or focused on what "everyone else is doing," then perhaps everything will feel like a struggle.

I know this mind state well since I've seen it in my own evolution moving from self-judgment, comparison to others leading to depression and moving more toward choosing healthy attitudes and behaviors that affirm and value my life. Choosing to be happy is something I do every day.

Our individual path to healing and happiness is a personal one, unique to each person and really the only thing we have control over. The only way to achieve peace starts within ourselves. Peace to me simply means feeling well. Not a temporary high from sugar, alcohol or a drug, but the healthy glow that comes from having a toolkit of wellness practices. When we are healthy, we are happy.

If we honestly examine our actions, then we can see how we are contributing to wellness or un-wellness. How we sustain ourselves, financially, energetically and on all levels, are increasingly important issues especially in the 21st century when resources are depleting and we, as a planet and people, face the ongoing threats of climate change [Ref. 8]. There's a lot to be aware of today, but if we begin with caring for ourselves, our families and our homes then I do believe life will align us more with what makes us whole and happy.

I love the word "awareness." Having the awareness that our survival depends on each other can give us a deeper respect for our lives, for others, for the generosity of the Earth. The root word of "awareness" is aware. My philosophy is that the "E" in "aware" stands for everyone, everything, everywhere. If we don't have the "E" in "aware" then we have "A War."

How can we have world peace if we are at war with ourselves? The way we treat ourselves is a reflection of what we value. And what we believe is reflected in how we live. Health to me, or achieving a state of wellness, is the start to world peace. Our lives are a tiny pebble dropped in a global pond that ripples out into our relationships, our community and the world at large.

Education is a lifelong journey. I believe the more we know, the more informed choices we can make to improve the quality of our lives in the most optimal way possible. Living without the dependency on chemicals or other habits that may be harmful to us is true liberation.

I do not claim to be an expert in anything but my own experience. And what may have worked for me may not work for others so I encourage you to always be the judge of what is right for you. My desire is to share what I have learned about how to achieve health and wellness so that you are informed and inspired on your own path of healing.

Walking the path of being one's own healer is a kind of modern-day self-shamanism. To deeply listen to our bodies and our spirits, letting them guide the body to what it needs. This is what I have come to understand through holistic health and choosing actions that help to maintain balance between my mind, body and spirit.

This book is a culmination of what has worked to help heal me in my life and what I am learning in the process of writing this book and I want to share that with you. I believe we always have a choice. Our choices reflect what we've been taught or what has been modeled to us, whether healthy or not.

My journey to creating health, happiness and peace has been a personal multi-faceted path of seeking the truth. Experience has always been my first teacher. And what is timeless will persist. Cultivating the practice of listening to my body has been paramount to this journey. Too often we ignore the messages our bodies are sending us, so I invite you to listen more deeply to the healer within.

Chapter 1

Know Thyself: Meditation as Medication

What is Reality?

Your mental state determines everything. "What you think, you become" says the Buddha. Our thoughts affect how we feel about ourselves, how we see others, how we see the world, how we understand our lives and whether we feel empowered to change our circumstance if we are unhappy or do nothing and become a victim to it.

Much of what we think or believe is shaped by what we are taught by our families and relationships, religion, education, society and the media, which we internalize over time and shape how we see ourselves. This can sometimes leave us feeling powerless and unhappy. How do we unlearn and relearn our ways of thinking and being, to feel more healthy, happy and self-empowered?

The ancient Greek philosopher Plato says "Reality is created by the mind. We can change our reality by changing our mind." Plato's work "Allegory of the Cave" is a metaphorical tale that investigates our human perception of reality, what we know, what we believe is truth and what it means to be free.

In this work, three prisoners are chained to a wall in a cave that they have lived in their entire lives. Their heads are tied so they cannot see anything but the wall in front of them. Behind them is a fire and a walkway where people perform, holding animals, plants and wood by the fire to cast shadows on the wall. The prisoners watch these images, thinking this is reality.

When one prisoner escapes, he sees the wonders of the physical world, a reality much more vibrant than the shadowy projections he had been watching. The sunlight burns his eyes, blinding him. He then understands the sun as the source of life and relishes in the beauty of the natural world outside of the cave. When he returns to the cave to share the news with his fellow prisoners, they shun him in disbelief and find comfort in the isolation of the cave.

The moral of the story is that our perception of reality is based on our experiences and values. The freed prisoner wanted to go beyond what he knew, to experience "true reality" and awakened to his own power. This inspired him to share his discovery with fellow prisoners so that they too could be free and experience a new reality.

Their negative reaction represents how some of us are content with living in the dark versus accepting what is real. Accepting what is real requires us to change. Real change requires a change in perception and a change in behavior.

To take full responsibility for ourselves is the only path to healing and transformation.

Self-reflection and self-examination can lead to self-discovery, freeing us to rewrite the story of our lives. This self-work is what makes our lives our own, helping us to find an inner happiness that no one can take away. Meditation is one way to achieve this or that is any activity that helps us become completely present, without past or future.

What is Happiness?

Every person has their own destiny, their own purpose. It's our work to discover what that is. When we work to fulfill this purpose, a deep fulfillment can keep us motivated to live. For some, their "why" is their children or their family.

For some it's obvious when we are young what our purpose is or what dreams are. Perhaps, it is because we are still pure, untainted by social conditioning of who we are or not supposed to be.

For me, I was always creative. I started singing at 3 years old. I began writing short stories and became an avid journaler by middle school. English was my favorite class because I got to express myself through my stories. This led to studying journalism, then taking an introduction class to film and I was hooked. I switched schools to study film, earned my degree in cinema then started a video production business shortly after.

Art was always my passion. When I pursued it, by making it my profession, it became my purpose in life that brings me great joy and fulfillment.

Michael Bernard Beckwith, author and spiritual director of the Agape International Spiritual Center, said in an interview with Ellen Degeneres that many people are unhappy not because of "attention deficit disorder" but of an "intention deficit disorder."

The word intention means, "to have a goal, purpose or aim." It also means the "healing of a wound." I think both of these definitions are true of what Beckwith is referring to.

To do the work of knowing ourselves and the self-discovery of our passion and purpose is the journey that makes our life our own. To have an "In"-tention, is to turn your attention within.

The art of self-reflection is one that will help you master yourself: to know yourself and what makes you happy is key. Having a passion that brings you joy will give back to you every time and is worthy of your time and attention to discover. Be curious and enjoy the process!

Happiness can come from many sources but when happiness comes from within you and not from an external source like a car, a substance or the approval of someone else, it is an absolute happiness independent of anything outside of you. This is self-empowerment and to me the essence of true happiness. To me, having an independent spirit like this is freedom.

There are almost 8 billion people in this world. Each person has their own path, purpose and unique struggles that define who they are. So is it not our birthright to decide what we believe and how we should live?

Living your "truth" according to you is what's most important as long as it doesn't harm anyone. Plato's Cave is about defining what is true for ourselves independent of what others think. This is key in maintaining our mental wellness and happiness.

This state of being centered and grounded was not always my normal state. And because of this, I was in a state of suffering. My center was in what my parents wanted, how other people perceived me and this practice of giving my power away to other people was commonplace. I was a victim. My happiness was dependent on things out of my control.

It's hard to win an argument with someone who is set on being the victim because nothing is ever their fault. Their suffering is the fault of their parents, a lover, societal oppression, a traumatic experience or whatever story they tell to keep them in victimhood. I know because this was me.

We all suffer as humans. But the moment we decide we are tired of suffering and want to be happy, we must take responsibility for our suffering and choose healthy ways to transform our pain into something positive.

This is when the universe will respond and support your happiness. It's the law of attraction. To move on solutions rather than be mired in your suffering by complaining or blaming, will begin to shift your life from victim to victor where now you are in the driver's seat of your life, not a passenger.

This is the point of meditation – to cultivate a centered, self-awareness of what will make you happy and to be self-empowered to choose the course of your life that will make you most happy. Of course, challenges will still arise but if you are in a place to face your life and not hide from it, that is the start of happiness.

The Buddha says "Be vigilant; guard your mind against negative thoughts." Meditation helps me to transform this toxic pattern of complaining, hiding on the sideline of my life and boldly get in the game of living my life. Being more self-aware and embodied in the present moment gets out of my head and grounded in my own experience.

I want to expand the idea of "meditation." It's not just sitting quietly, breathing and observing one's thoughts. To me, meditation is any healthy activity that gets into a meditative state, not in the past and future, but completely in the moment.

"The Power of Now" by Eckhart Tolle is an amazing book that promotes the liberating perspective of living in the present moment. He states on being present, "Life is now. There was never a time when your life was not now, nor will there ever be" [Ref.

111]. Tolle also affirms the limits of the mind by saying, "You also realize that all the things that truly matter - beauty, love, creativity, joy, and inner peace - arise from beyond the mind" [Ref. 111].

What Shapes Our Mental Health?

Our mental health is connected to our lifestyle choices. By employing a wide range of modalities to transform our suffering into wellness in addition to a solid foundation of eating a nutritious diet, getting adequate sleep, regular exercise and sunlight exposure, can really improve our mental state.

While there are some mental health problems that can be clinical and may require medical treatment, I do believe there is much we can do on our own as well to mitigate our own suffering. In the cases of deep trauma, there are also ancient ways, indigenous people have healed themselves with psychoactive plant medicines, which I explore in my entheogens chapter.

Mental health is a matter of having a healthy perspective of ourselves. By remaining curious, we can discover ways in which we can better care for ourselves by freeing and healing our minds, moving our bodies while establishing and maintaining our peace in healthy, sustainable ways.

Creativity, meditation, journaling, heart to heart dialogue, nature time, yoga, dancing, movement and sports are just some of the ways I enjoy to achieve mental wellness.

With mental health, much of our issues can derive from some form of trauma we have experienced. Trauma that has not yet been fully processed, integrated and healed.

Trauma can be experienced from childhood and family issues, shame, guilt, abuse, violence, war, discrimination, poverty, oppression, neglect, accidents, illness, loss of relationships and family and a whole host of issues that cause humans to suffer.

Integration is the process through which we begin to seek a deeper understanding of our experiences, and to be accountable for the behaviors and tendencies behind the actions we are choosing, so that we can shift our lifestyle choices to live more holistically, more intentionally, leading to greater health and happiness. There are many ways we can achieve this which I will explore.

The most important thing is to be patient with ourselves in the process of healing our trauma. To understand that we are all unique and that our path to healing may look different and that that is normal.

I believe the underlying cause of addiction, toxic behavior and unhealthy relationships is unresolved trauma. We all have endured trauma, so how do we begin to heal?

Talk therapy is one route that some have found success in healing past traumas. Processing our painful experiences with a trusted professional can be useful in helping to understand our emotions, unhealthy habits, and identify the underlying trauma that may have caused these patterns so that we can change our behavior.

But if you are unable to afford such services, I do believe we can achieve healing through other modalities like meditation, yoga, self-reflection, a healthy diet, exercise, heart-to-heart dialogue with the support of trusted friends and family and other activities that can help us heal.

I have tried talk therapy several times and learned some insightful tools to help alleviate what I was going through. When I was in a romantic partnership, we went to couples therapy and gained some useful tools on how to communicate more fairly like starting our dialogues with gratitude and using a talking stone to ensure that one person spoke at a time. It was useful for me at that moment.

However, I did not find talk therapy to be the best fit for me in my healing process since I did not like how the sessions were so short, typically 45 minutes. Just as I was starting to get into my issues, the session would be over which felt unsatisfying and that it did not go deep enough. Not to mention, it can cost up to $100 an hour or more.

If you can afford it and it works for you, go for it. Like I said, healing will look different for different people. Always listen to yourself first and do what works for you.

The limitation of talk therapy is that it deals with healing trauma through the limits of words and the mind. I found by accessing the wisdom of the body and spirit to be the best medicine that has helped me on my healing journey.

Movement, Exercise and Embodiment

Movement activities like dancing and running helps me to release my mind which is incredibly therapeutic and necessary for balance. When we move and sweat, we produce endorphins, our brain's feel-good neurotransmitters. Even just walking 20-30 minutes a day or more has a whole host of benefits like preventing disease.

The point is to balance the mind and body with healthy sustainable solutions. Alcohol, drugs and other forms of release may help temporarily but not if they leave you feeling toxic afterwards.

By staying active with regular exercise just three times a week or walking everyday, you can release the stress of the mind, uplift your mood and go deeper into the moment to achieve a relaxed state and deeper peace. Dancing, biking, hiking and yoga are my personal favorites.

The dance floor is my church. Dancing is when I feel most free. Moving to soulful house music makes me breathe, sweat and move while communing with others. Letting the healing power of music wash over me is very healing and liberating to me like a sound bath for my soul. When I immerse myself in the rhythm of the sound, I create patterns with my body and I release my worries and find the simple joy of being alive.

Physical movement, dancing, yoga, breathwork, massage, orgasms, exercise and sports are just some amazing outlets to get out of our minds and into our bodies, into the present moment. The mind and ego can have a very limited view of our full human experience. So don't believe everything your mind thinks, especially when you don't feel well or are in a bad mood.

Somatic therapy or body psychotherapy helps to move trauma that gets stored in the body from painful experiences we may have. There are a number of techniques practitioners use to help people identify where pain lives in their body and by using breath and awareness can move and release stuck energy.

Floatation therapy tanks along with sensory deprivation also have similar benefits like stress and pain reduction, improved sleep and increased focus.

19
Meditation, Self-Reflection and Integration Practices

Having a self-care routine is key in maintaining mental health. My mind, body and spirit must be in balance and harmony to achieve wellness. Spirituality is a big part of feeling well and my self-care practice.

Our spirits are the foundation of our very existence. Spirit is what animates our flesh. Do you believe in reincarnation? Or that the soul or spirit is eternal?

When people say, you have an old soul or have a soulmate, then that's what that means, that you have been here before in another form in relation to others who you are connected to like your family, lovers, etc.

I have seen spirit leave the body of loved ones and felt their presence later. Or the unexplained familiarity of a place or person I have encountered for the first time...This is how I know spirit is eternal.

Accessing the infinite source of spirit, through spiritual practices like meditation and prayer open the possibility to a deeper healing that feels the most effective, holistic and sustainable to me.

I come from a devout Catholic family where we attended church every Sunday and had an altar in our house with over 30 figures of various deities. Having strong faith and praying daily was normal to me. Now I have just translated this spiritual discipline to Nichiren Buddhism which fits my beliefs and values more.

Our bodies exist in the third dimension: our physical reality. When we achieve a meditative state or are in deep prayer, we access the fifth dimension, the spirit dimension.

Maybe you are not a "spiritual person," but how do you explain coincidences or being led to people and places that help you when you are in need. Call it God or the universe, but there is an intelligence working on your behalf whether you are aware of it or not.

Ancient Chinese philosopher, founder of Taoism or Daoism and writer of the Tao Te Ching, Lao Tzu, says "If you are depressed you are living in the past. If you are anxious you are living in the future. If you are at peace you are living in the present."

Daoists believe in the unity, harmony and balance of all opposing forces, which is where the ancient symbol of the yin yang comes from. They also believed that the spirit which animates all life is eternal and returns to the source when one dies. This philosophy encourages compassion, simplicity and patience and where the term "go with the flow" is derived. It is a wonderful philosophy to apply to one's life to create more balance and peace in our busy modern lives.

There are many forms of ancient meditation practices to achieve wellness that are free and just require your focused effort. The point is to achieve a state of mindfulness and awareness; by focusing on the breath or the repetition of a mantra.

Meditation is powerful because it accesses the infinite reservoir of the spirit through focused breath. To inspire, in its Latin roots and other languages means to "in spirit" or "breathe into." We are given a body which has form and the mind which is formless. Through the breath, we can bridge and integrate both form and formlessness into harmony and balance.

Yoga, meditation, creativity and other integration tools can bring about a meditative state fostering inspiration and more holistic ways of experiencing a deeper healing.

Silent meditation finds its roots in Hinduism and Buddhism. It is the practice of sitting still with eyes closed or relaxed, bringing one's awareness to the breath and sensations of the body to release the mind. With steady practice one can gain self-awareness, and witness the thoughts of the mind without attaching to them. This state of detachment through observation can help us be more present and embodied.

Our suffering is usually caused by zooming in like a microscope on one detail or a negative perception of a situation. When we achieve detachment, or what I call the "bird's eye" view, we can zoom out and see the whole picture. It can offer clarity on the lesson a situation is teaching us or develop more compassion for ourselves or others involved.

Our minds can be busy with recurring thoughts, judgments and our stories that we project on reality, but with detachment it allows us the space to allow thoughts to come and go. This state of objective observation without judgment or identifying with every thought can bring a state of mindfulness and deeper peace.

In Buddhism, they say "attachment is suffering." When we attach to people, material things and specific outcomes we suffer. This goes hand in hand with another Buddhist principle, impermanence, which is the state or fact that all things only exist for a limited amount of time.

It is the understanding that our lives, our youth or anything that lives will one day expire or end. Being in a state of detachment acknowledges this universal principle of impermanence to help us mitigate our suffering.

Tibetan Buddhists create colorful, elaborate mandalas made of sand to represent the structure of the universe; the center is where the gods dwell. They spend days creating a beautiful mandala only afterwards to destroy it by sweeping it aside in moments. This meditation is an example of cultivating a detachment and reverence for the principle of impermanence that moves in all of our lives.

The oldest form of silent meditation to become popularized is called a Vipassana or "seeing things just as they are" retreat. It gained popularity in the 1950s among monks in Burma then American Buddhist teachers like Jack Kornfield, Sharon Salzberg and others began to spread its practice to the US and abroad.

It is the practice of staying in silent meditation for ten days and its roots go back before the Buddha's time. Many practitioners say they gain greater clarity, peace and a deeper embodiment of the present moment. You can find Vipassana centers across the US and the world now.

In my twenties, I struggled with insecurity and wanted to find ways to build my confidence, ground my energy and calm my emotions when I was feeling challenged. I searched for a teacher for months and encountered a silent meditation teacher which was helpful to a degree, but still did not help me achieve my goals.

Then one day at Earth Dance Festival, a transformational arts festival in the San Francisco Bay area, one of my soul sisters sat me down to recite gongyo and daimoku, chapters from the Myoho Renge Kyo sutra by the original Buddha. These are the meditative practices of Nichiren Buddhism led by Soka-Gakkai International also known as SGI from Japan.

As soon as I started to recite the prayers, I knew this was the tool I had been searching for. Little did I know that this practice would completely revolutionize my life—improving my confidence, finances, family relationships and more.

I first heard of "Nam myoho renge kyo" in the film, "What's Love Got To Do With It?" starring Angela Bassett. There is a scene where she is holding beads and repeating the mantra while hitting a bell. This was the practice she used to heal herself and release her from the toxic relationship she was in with Ike Turner, so I knew it must be a powerful mantra with transformative abilities.

Reciting the mantra has the power of "changing poison into medicine," which I have witnessed in my life and others. I have seen practitioners use chanting to transform divorce, addiction, cancer, AIDS and into a positive outcome.

"Nam myoho renge kyo" is based on the Mystic Law of Cause and Effect from Nichiren Buddhism. Repeating the mantra activates your Buddha nature and the light within you. Chanting is the true cause we can make for living our best life. The chanting of the mantra or daimoku (meaning "light") raises our life condition to the tenth world of Buddhahood.

In the words of our mentor, Daisaku Ikeda, "[Buddhahood] is the joy of joys. Birth, old age, illness and death are no longer suffering, but part of the joy of living. The light of wisdom illuminates the entire universe, casting back the innate darkness of life" [Ref 5].

The Ten Worlds are the four lower worlds: hell, hunger, animality and anger. The six noble worlds or higher states of consciousness are humanity, heaven, learning, self-realization, bodhisattva and buddhahood [Ref 6]. The Ten Worlds is a powerful concept that helped me to understand the various life conditions or mind states that we could be at any given moment.

Through the power of chanting, we can raise our life condition to the Buddha state or to view our lives from the "bird's eye" view to help us our lives with greater clarity and understanding. When we activate our Buddhahood by chanting "nam myoho renge kyo," we create our environment into "the land of Eagle Peak" or a place of ascension where compassion, wisdom and understanding creates an absolute happiness found within ourselves.

Nichiren Buddhists believe that this Buddha state can be achieved through chanting this mantra and is available to anyone. In literal terms, Nam myoho renge kyo means "Devotion to the Mystic Law of Cause and Effect Through Sound, Teaching and Vibration." The power of the mantra is most potent in the experiential meaning of the words.

Chanting this mantra has two benefits; one is known as "conspicuous" benefits or material benefits like finding a new house, job, car or relationship and the other is known as "inconspicuous" benefits which are more internal like achieving more clarity, confidence, strength and peace.

For me, the humanistic principles of Nichiren Buddhism of equality and self-empowerment was a breath of fresh air after being raised Catholic which has a lot of judgmental views around women and gay people, which I am both. Chanting helped me feel empowered to be who I fully am.

The result of chanting this mantra consistently can achieve an "absolute happiness" or a happiness that stems from within us, not outside of us which is considered "relative happiness." It helps us to live from our fullest potential and spread world peace or what is known as "kosen-rufu."

My experience of Catholicism was based on the belief that humans are inherently guilty, as seen in the concept of "original sin" or being a sinner. Many prayers I recited were about asking for forgiveness. The viewpoint of God being superior and outside of us with absolute power to help or punish us to me felt wrong and disempowering.

By chanting, I feel liberated and encouraged to expand my spirit and explore my mind to find the light and wisdom within myself and my own experiences first, rather than outside of myself.

As a singer and DJ/musician, I also resonate with chanting. Through the use of sound and the power of our voice, we can move the universe in the direction of our desires. The universe is in fact made of sound. If you look at the smallest particles of matter, atoms, they are mostly empty space. This empty space is vibrating at such a high frequency that it is solid. This vibrating empty space can also be likened to sound.

Chanting this mantra can change "poison into medicine" as I have witnessed it in my own life and in other's lives. This means whatever challenge or negative karma we have, we can change it into a positive outcome. I love this because we can see our suffering as fuel for our happiness.

When we chant, we use our voice for a prolonged amount of time, which starts to move all the chakras, or energy centers in our body, generating more power and energy in our beings. By building confidence, courage and motivation through chanting, I was able to take action and transform my situation for the better.

Through self-examination, we can grow and improve. By detaching ourselves from our past stories from the past and becoming present, we can rewrite the story into what we want to see for our future. To find solutions to our problems, I believe it is best to consult ourselves or others that have gone through similar circumstances.

Journaling was one of my first mental health tools as an adolescent. Writing down how I felt helped me process and make sense of what was happening in my life at that moment. By documenting our life experiences, we can also look back at it, at a later time to see how much we have grown or not grown. This insight is invaluable and can also serve as a wealth of experiences to draw from when we are creating art, be it writing songs, stories, and more.

Self-reflection through journaling is key in discovering our inner power, finding our own voice and unique path to healing, by gaining a deeper understanding of who we are. When something that stresses you is put on paper then it has less power over and lets you gain perspective of the experience, rather than suffering because of it.

Inner child work or inner child healing, is a powerful, meditative tool that helps us dive deeper into our "shadow self" or our subconscious mind.

Our subconscious mind takes up 90-95% of our mind and contains all of our "programming" of what we think, what we believe and the reasons why we react to things the way we do. This means that our conscious mind or that which is in our present awareness only takes up 10% of our mind. From this standpoint, we can see why it's so hard to change our patterns.

I did some inner child work with a practitioner, and she helped me uncover some deeper childhood traumas that were affecting my relationship patterns. From there, I was able to use the tool on my own through journaling and meditation. It has helped me go deeper into understanding myself, unlearning patterns that no longer serve me and rewriting my story in a way that supports my health and happiness.

Artistic expression is an effective way to transform our suffering into a work of art that can illuminate the wisdom we gain from going through our unique challenges. The magic of art is that when we share it, even people from a different background can find the universal truth. This is the power of storytelling as a means to bring people together and serves as a form of healing for all of us.

Nature Is Our Sanctuary

Hiking or spending time in nature is vital to healing. Also referred to as ecotherapy, it is well documented that nature heals. The Earth is our home. We depend on the Earth to provide us with air, water, food and all the resources needed for living. We easily take for granted how our fuel for our vehicles, energy grids and machines, all rely on the Earth and human labor.

We can develop an attitude of gratitude by simply appreciating our planet's bounty and beauty. For most of us, especially those living in cities, our connection to nature and the Earth has been severed, making depression more commonplace.

Nature heals us through unity. When you enter a park, forest, or shore, nature simply welcomes you and allows you to just be.

There is no ego, no competition, no stress. Nature is like being in the complete acceptance and support of a loving mother. We move and breathe in fresh oxygen from the trees, soak up the warmth and vitamin D from sunlight and are exhilarated by the wind or water on our skin. Nature revitalizes our senses and stirs our entire being. It's an amazing healer that we can usually access for free.

Having places and spaces that are welcoming like nature, being in the embrace of blood and spirit families, our communities, groups of shared interests and cultural gatherings that bring people together is also vital to mental health.

When you are living in the city, there are concrete streets, walls and doors that separate us from each other. Constantly being in this environment can cause isolation and disconnection that can lead to depression and mental health issues. Being in an overpopulated city, also requires us to compete for jobs, money and resources. It requires us to create boundaries between ourselves and others for safety. This constant state of being in competition, guarded and vigilant can also affect our mental wellness.

Finding nature anywhere you live, especially in an urban environment is vital to mental wellness. Just being near water is shown to improve feelings of happiness, health and peace.

Knowing yourself and what your needs are will be vital to choosing the best environment to live in for your own mental health. Having a ritual to maintain your balance and peace is possible to cultivate in any environment. It requires some exploration to know what practices will bring your being into balance. Enjoy the process! The payoff is vital in being able to maintain your own happiness and increase the longevity of your life.

Yoga: The Ancient Practice of Breathing into Balance

Yoga was refined and developed by Rishis (sages) who documented their practices and beliefs in the Upanishads, a huge work containing over 200 scriptures. Yoga is amongst the six schools of philosophy in Hinduism, and is also a major part of Buddhism and its meditation practices and can be dated over 5,000 years ago based on the sacred text, Rig Veda, from Northern India.

To me, yoga is one of the most powerful tools of spirit integration, connecting the mind and body through breath. Combining physical and spiritual practices, yoga creates harmony between the body and mind through ancient asanas or postures that tap into the vast reservoir of the spirit. It can bring about improved concentration, self-awareness, circulation, core strength, flexibility, weight loss, increased immunity, better sleep, digestion, relaxation and so much more. I cannot recommend yoga enough as a practice to bring about more healing and wellness into your life.

There are many forms of yoga but some of the most popular are: Hatha yoga, Vinyasa yoga, Power yoga, Ashtanga yoga, hot yoga, Iyengar yoga, Kundalini yoga and Restorative yoga. Hatha yoga is great for beginners with a focus on how to breathe, relax and meditate. Vinyasa yoga is a dynamic flow of postures that flow into one another creating seamless movement, ideal for active, restless and creative people who want to move. Power yoga is a fast-paced version of Vinyasa, focused on burning calories and building strength and endurance. Ashtanga yoga, known as the yoga of warriors, is the most demanding, designed to increase the body's endurance, strength and helpful for weight loss and stress relief.

Hot yoga is the practice of yoga in a heated room from 80-100 degrees which increases calorie burning, flexibility and eliminating toxins. It was popularized by Indian yogi, Bikram Choudhury, in the 1970s. However, due to his multiple sexual assault allegations filed against him from female students, I want to acknowledge that men in power who abuse their positions by taking advantage of others is wrong, so I do not support Bikram. There are many other yoga studios that teach hot yoga. When I took hot vinyasa in Virginia at a great studio called Siri Om Yoga, after an hour of class I was soaked in sweat. Afterwards, I would take a shower and feel like I had a brand new body. Hot yoga is the ultimate detox if you are a fan of the sauna and yoga combined.

Iyengar yoga focuses on the correct alignment of the spine to improve posture and is ideal for those who have suffered injuries, the elderly or those just beginning. The postures are executed slowly increasing flexibility, posture and body toning. Kundalini yoga is more spiritual, focusing on meditation and postures that awaken the kundalini or energy around the spine.

The postures are done repeatedly creating an intensity that can move blocked energy in the back and hips which are areas we hold trauma. Some students find themselves in tears after some of these poses as they release blocked energy that we may have been holding onto without even knowing, therefore we can experience a deep psychological healing from this practice. Restorative yoga is focused on gentle, passive postures that soothes the nervous system, promotes deeper relaxation and can achieve a meditative state without breaking a sweat.

Our Mind is a Garden: Plant Seeds of Positivity

Positive affirmations, visualization and vision boards are also great tools to manifest what we want in our lives. Everything happens twice, once within our minds then in real life. We must clear our minds of fear and doubt to manifest the lives we dream of. Just as we may have been conditioned to believe erroneous teachings about our self-worth and what we are capable of, that may cripple us with fear, we can retrain the mind to believe in new paradigms that are empowering and healing.

Self-talk is key in transforming our lives and creating the best lives. Change your mind, change your life. The power of words can absolutely transform our lives, written, spoken or heard within. I generate my own affirmations from my own personal struggles. I use the power of words as an antidote to life's challenges.

My motto is always to consult yourself first but sometimes we all need some help and inspiration. There are many great affirmation books out there by amazing writers like Louise Hay and Iyanla Vanzant to name a few. Louise Hay's "You Can Heal Your Life," from 1984 is still a classic. One line from her book, "When we create peace and harmony and balance in our minds, we will find it in our lives."

This is my intention with this book. I believe the state we cultivate within our own lives ripples out into our relationships and into the world. When we do the work on ourselves, we will see and feel the results in our lives. Iyanla Vanzant's "Acts of Faith" is a classic written over 25 years ago and is a compilation of daily affirmations sensitive to the struggles of people of color to encourage, comfort and enlighten readers.

Our internal speech to ourselves is everything. The first 20 minutes after awakening, our brains are in a theta state of focus and deep relaxation found when in prayer, meditation or during a creative activity [Ref. 101]. It is said that the mind is most impressionable at this time. This is a great time to read positive affirmations, before sleeping or anytime really. We become what we think.

I like to write my own affirmations as medicine to whatever I am dealing with at the time. Affirmations are present-tense positive reminders of what to focus our minds on. By repeatedly focusing our minds on these points of energy helps to bring them into reality. Saying them aloud is also a powerful practice of manifestation. Then, we need to take action from these mindsets to fully realize our goals.

There are many other forms of chanting meditations, affirmations, writing down goals and creating vision boards that can orient the mind toward success, health and happiness. In "Being Mary Jane" a TV drama that follows a successful TV news anchor; played by Gabrielle Union, she has little sticky notes with positive affirmations all over her apartment to get her mindset right.

The mind is a powerful tool so what we put into it – whether it is negative or positive – will have a magnifying effect. The Buddha says, "Be vigilant; guard your mind against negative thoughts." So if we want to manifest our desires, it is our self-work to fill it with positive thoughts and release the fear and doubt of others and our environment. Happiness is a choice. This is what it means when we say I am choosing to be happy.

<u>Chapter 1: Reflections</u>:
What wellness activities do you do to maintain your mental health? How can you improve?

Chapter 2

Heal Thyself: Naturopathy, Food as Medicine

The Connection Between Food and Health

Growing up Filipino American, I was raised on a typical American diet of fast food, sugary sodas, lots of wheat gluten in bread, pasta, pizza and donuts, along with lots of dairy foods like milk, cheese and ice cream.

I also inherited the Filipino tradition of eating a white rice and meat heavy diet. We ate lots of pork, the meat highest in sodium and fat content, with very little to no vegetables in sight. I subsisted just fine on these foods until my body began to break down and have problems.

It was a blessing in disguise because it led me to an awakening about nutrition.

I have many relatives, including my sister, who have eaten this "typical" diet all their lives. They are obese, some weighing over 300 pounds and have a host of health issues. Sadly, they were not taught to understand the connection between food and health. This is why I have written this book. I want them—and everyone—to know that we have a choice if we want a better quality of life. In fact, all diet related illnesses and deaths are preventable.

An older cousin I grew up with, was fond of eating a Filipino dish called, "chicharron bulaklak," which translates to "deep fried pork flowers." Also known as "chitterlings or chitlins" in African American culture which is deep fried pig intestines. My cousin had a mild stroke at the age of 30 that caused brain damage and left him disabled. He was lucky to survive, but sadly, his stroke was possibly preventable.

White rice is a Filipino staple, served at every meal and the basis of a lot of Filipino desserts. The desserts are delicious but when I eat them I feel like there's a rock in my gut. As I came of age, I moved away from this diet as I noticed how tired eating foods like this made me feel.

Then I observed that my mother, grandmother, three of her sisters, including my older sister, have all died from complications due to type 2 diabetes. Studies show that type 2 diabetes is linked to a high consumption of white rice that causes spikes in blood sugar levels [Ref 16].

I told this to my mother and sister while they were alive but they said what do I know since I was not a doctor. May they rest in peace. But when doctors don't tell their patients about the link between food and disease because they are trained to prescribe drugs, we have to self-educate to find more effective solutions to improve our health.

You know the food system is broken when chemical-laden, artificial foods are cheaper than fresh food that comes from the ground. People say that eating healthy is expensive. While this is true at first glance especially if you go to expensive stores like Whole Foods, another way to look at it is what you pay now for healthy eating, will save you later than becoming ill from eating poorly and have to pay high medical bills.

You can also shop for whole foods at local farmers' markets, local grocers who support local growers, join a community garden or better yet grow your own food. If you live in cities without land, there are many container set-ups to grow food on your roof, fire escape or wall gardens which are becoming more popular now.

If you are on a budget, you can also go to the Chinatown, local Asian or Latino food store. I find these communities charge less at blue-collar prices. They may not always be organic but sometimes you can find some at great prices.

My first awakening that food and health were related was when I moved to the San Francisco Bay Area when I was 21. My vegetarian roommate had a cook book explaining that many American foods contain chemicals called GMOs or "genetically modified organisms," also known as "genetically engineered"or "bioengineered" foods. The chemical structure of GMOs to plastic is identical. It was the first time I had ever heard of this. Genetically modified foods have been modified in a lab so they can last longer to make more profit.

In addition to US food corporations like Monsanto, Bayer, Dupont and Dow Chemical, genetically modifying food crops, foods are also treated with harmful herbicides like glyphosate. So when you consume GMOs, you are eating the pesticides used to treat them. According to the Journal of Organic Systems, the consumption of GMOs is linked to over 22 diseases including gastrointestinal disorders, obesity, diabetes, heart disease, depression, autism, infertility, cancer and Alzheimer's disease [Ref 17,18].

A great documentary called, "What's With Wheat?" written by nutritionist, Cyndi O'Meara; goes into depth about the glyphosate treated GMO, wheat and its connection to the rise of gluten intolerance, celiac disease, multiple sclerosis, asthma, rheumatoid arthritis and more [Ref 19].

Later I discovered that I was gluten and dairy intolerant. Once I eliminated this from my diet, I found my digestion greatly improved. Now I eat a more plant-based diet with eating gluten or dairy occasionally and my body is way more balanced now.

Our Bodies Can Heal Themselves

"You are what you eat," is a cliche but also accurate. The amazing divine creation we understand as the human body has the capacity to heal itself. When we get a cut, we take for granted that tiny red blood cells gather together to create collagen and heal our skin.

Every organ, tissue, muscle, bone and cell is manufactured from what we eat. So a bowl of yogurt with granola and blueberries will help us stay healthy, unlike if we ate an artificially flavored blueberry toaster pastry.

The Greek physician, Hippocrates, is known as the father of modern medicine. He wrote over 70 books on diseases and their treatment after detailed observation. He believed in holistic health and the use of natural food and remedies to activate the body's capacity to heal itself.

According to Stanford Medicine, doctors receive little to no education on nutrition in medical school or about 2 hours in the span of 10-14 years of schooling. When doctors are sworn in, they take the "Hippocratic Oath." [Ref. 2] The oath is based on the work of Hippocrates, who said, "Let food be thy medicine, and let medicine be thy food."

The irony is that Hippocrates believed in the healing power of nature and that illnesses could be healed by changing one's diet, environmental factors and living habits. He believed the body has the ability to heal itself and that it was the physician's job only to 'facilitate natural healing.' In fact, he believed that the worst thing a physician could do was interfere with the body's natural healing power." [Ref 9]

So if Hippocrates was really a naturopath and practiced holistic medicine, why aren't doctors armed with the knowledge of nutrition as a viable method of healing illnesses? Clearly modern-day health care in the US has veered away from what its founder intended. Why is this so?

The History of the U.S. Medical System Business Model

In the 19th century, natural cures were a common form of treatment in hospitals and medical schools. But by the mid-20th century they became non-existent. This was due to the Flexner Report, written by Abraham Flexner, that discredited holistic health and natural medicine practices to Congress in 1910 [Ref. 36]. The report concluded that "there are too many doctors and medical schools in America, and that all the natural healing modalities which had existed for hundreds of years were unscientific quackery" [Ref. 37]. Homeopathy and natural medicines were mocked and demonized, and doctors were even jailed [Ref. 28].

Flexner's work was commissioned by the Carnegie Foundation and funded by John D. Rockerfeller [Ref. 28]. Rockefeller was America's first billionaire; he monopolized the oil industry, owning over 90% of it. His business, Standard Oil Corporation, later split into Exxon, Mobil and Chevron [Ref. 28].

At this time in the early 1900s scientists discovered vitamins and pharmaceutical drugs could be made from petrochemicals as well [Ref. 28]. Rockerfeller saw this as an opportunity to control and monopolize multiple industries: petroleum, chemical and medical.

Petrochemicals were ideal from a business perspective because they could be patented, owned and sold for high profits [Ref. 37].

There was however big competition to his plan as natural and herbal medicines were very popular at the time. Rockerfeller turned to fellow billionaire Andrew Carnegie for advice and the Flexner Report was born [Ref. 28]. It was at this time, where the term "a pill for an ill," became the standard for how to treat illness.

According to Zippia, which employs over 42,000 experts, the US pharmaceutical industry's revenue grew from $291 billion in 2010 to $425 billion in 2020. They state "41% of Americans say they have a fair amount or a great deal of trust in pharmaceutical companies to look out for their best interests [Ref. 115]." While the CDC, Center for Disease Control and Prevention, reports that "drug overdose deaths in the U.S. are up 30% in 2020 [Ref. 116]."

The Lown Institute states, "the practice of polypharmacy has increased by 200% in over 20 years where 42% of older adults take 5 or more prescription medications" [Ref. 12] which I witnessed with my parents. Polypharmacy in older adults has resulted in "$62 billion of medical costs in unnecessary hospitalizations over 10 years" [Ref. 12].

Corporate greed for profits is a driving force in modern medicine whether we like it or not. Doctors are pressured to meet a quota of prescribing medications, ordering tests, filling beds and admitting patients from the emergency room and those over 65 years of age to increase profits [Ref 10].

The pharmaceutical industry has followed a brilliant two-pronged strategy to maximize profits: raise prices and increase consumption of medications [Ref 11]. According to the Lown Institute, medication overload will contribute to the premature deaths of

150,000 older Americans over the next decade and reduce the quality of life for millions more [Ref 12].

I saw this in my own household growing up. My mother and sister suffered from diabetes and hypertension. My father suffered from high blood pressure as well, resulting in a heart attack. They were all on a laundry list of medications.

They took these medications faithfully every day. My sister did not take her medications regularly nor did she ever try to reduce her high sugar intake, and diabetes ultimately took her life at 54. It always felt wrong to see my parents take all these chemicals that gave them a poor quality of life. I knew there had to be another way to heal these chronic issues beyond medications.

In my opinion, Western allopathic medicine or reactive medicine is great at dealing with medical emergencies like a broken bone, a heart attack, a ruptured spleen or any issue requiring immediate attention. However, the allopathic treatment of chronic illnesses like diabetes, high blood pressure, digestive issues and inflammatory issues like arthritis fails with pharmaceutical drugs . Why?

Naturopathic medicine or preventative medicine goes to the root cause of a chronic issue and nips it in the bud. Whereas, taking prescription medicines take away your symptoms but cause side effects and still not address the underlying cause of the illness. Can you heal chronic illness with drugs? In my experience, having family members who died in the care of that medical system, the answer is no.

According to Cancer Research UK, "1 in 2 people will get cancer in their lifetime - one of the main reasons for this being that people are living longer. Half of all cancers are in people over the age of 70" [Ref. 117]. The WHO, World Health Organization, says cancer is the leading cause of death. The go-to treatment for cancer is chemotherapy and radiotherapy. Both of which are toxic treatments that kill not just the cancerous cells but the healthy ones too, causing many undesirable side effects while lowering your immunity system, so the body's ability to fight off infection is greatly reduced. In the medical system, there is no other choice offered.

I had a dear friend who was diagnosed with stage 3 cancer in her 30s. She was beautiful and vibrant at the time. She went to the doctor and was given the only route to heal which was with toxic chemicals and radiation. Friends watched her wither away. Her beautiful energy was diminished and her hair fell out, a common side effect of chemo. She died a few months later. Did she die from chemo or from cancer? I will always wonder.

In addition to chemo's health risks, on average it also costs between $10,000-200,000 (with some exceeding $1 million) without health insurance and about 10-15 % of that with insurance [Ref. 118]. Not to mention, the money one loses by not working while undergoing treatment and recovery. A poll conducted by KFF (Kaiser Family Foundation), about two-thirds of adults with health care debt had cancer or someone in their family and had to drastically change their lifestyle (if and) once they survived the disease while "about 1 in 4 declared bankruptcy or lost their home from eviction or foreclosure" [Ref. 119].

Do you still think it's expensive to eat well and live healthy?

Gerson Therapy is a natural treatment of healing cancer developed by Max Gerson in the 1940s. Dr. Gerson identified that cancer develops when changes in cell metabolism are caused when the body is overloaded with toxins from unhealthy foods, addictions or the environment and the liver becomes overworked [Ref. 120].

The approach is based on traditional medicine of healing with a diet of organic fruits, vegetables and whole grains, low in sodium and high in potassium, to provide the body with plenty of vitamins, minerals and nutrients to activate the body's own healing capacity. Through supplements and detoxification, the body is rebalanced to help correct cell metabolism and remove toxic substances from the body [Ref. 120].

There are numerous health centers that offer Gerson Therapy, all over the world typically set in a natural environment which is a part of the healing process. At the Hawaii Naturopathic Retreat under the care of Dr. Baylac, there are numerous testimonials of people with all types of cancer that have healed naturally with this method. People who changed their lifestyle to heal from chronic illness and afterwards live better lives because they have taken responsibility for their health by making better choices.

Gerson Therapy is not a popular route to healing cancer, just research what the FDA says. But if you read the testimonials of successful cases or if you have ever healed yourself of an illness with natural foods like I have, then you are living proof that it can and does work.

Naturopathy: Healing with Natural Foods, Plants & Hydration

"Supersize Me" is a documentary where filmmaker Morgan Spurlock conducts an experiment by only eating food from McDonalds for a month. His health and libido decline and he gains over 20 pounds. He leaves some french fries out for two months and they never decompose. He illustrates that processed and genetically modified fast foods also stay in your body, causing negative health issues.

If artificial foods stay in the body longest, then the job of natural foods is to nourish the body and clear it of toxins. It's not fiction, it's science.

One of my health mentors, Master Wang, explained that Western medicine is based on allopathic medicine, which is concerned with treating the symptoms of an illness with drugs, radiation and surgery. Whereas naturopathy is the use of natural modalities like herbs, nutrition, massage, acupuncture, exercise, etc. to activate the body's own natural ability to heal itself and stay healthy.

Master Wang was a naturopathic practitioner and healer of traditional Chinese and Tibetan medicine. These ancient healing practices go back to over 3,000 years; they use natural herbs, foods and minerals to treat a variety of ailments.

Modern medicine and the use of pharmaceutical drugs to treat illnesses began in the 18th century about 300 years old. The largest difference in treatment is that modern medicine is derived from chemicals that cause side effects and traditional medicine derived from plants typically have no side effects.

Plant-based diets, herbs and whole foods are more gentle than chemicals to heal our bodies, because they are able to activate the body's own pharmacy and ability to heal itself. Plant foods contain more than 5,000 phytonutrients that detox the body, reduce chronic inflammation, balance hormones and produce an antioxidant effect (Ref. 188). A plant-based diet increases the body's own immunity to diseases.

The power of naturopathy or traditional medicine became clear to me three times before I became a true believer in the healing power of nature. When I was 21, I moved from Chicago to the San Francisco Bay Area and for the first time I had experienced allergies with hay fever symptoms. Being raised American, I turned to over-the-counter drugs like Benadryl to treat my runny nose and sneezing. This became costly in becoming dependent on a drug while also dealing with the side effects of a stomach ache or headache.

Thankfully, my new home, the Bay area, is known for its naturopathic healing community. So I checked out Rainbow Grocery, a natural food market in San Francisco, for an alternative to the drugs I was taking. At Rainbow Grocery, I found a host of natural remedies, including a tincture made from herbs to help alleviate allergies.

Low and behold after taking the tincture for a week, my symptoms went away and never returned. I was amazed. Not only did it work, but it also activated my body's immunity to the allergens to the point where I no longer needed it. Naturopathy is liberating. When you can find a natural remedy to heal an illness, it frees you from the yoke of being dependent on a drug.

The second time naturopathy trumped allopathy for me was when I was in my late 20s when I got my first full time job with benefits. I had more money to spend so I could eat out at restaurants more and I also had health insurance. My diet consisted of spicy food, fried foods and I loved a beer or glass of wine with it. Up to that point, I don't recall ever having any digestive issues, eating usually whatever I wanted without any problems. I remember at that time, having a busier schedule I would drink coffee in the mornings sometimes on an empty stomach.

After months of living with this diet and lifestyle, I started to experience intense heartburn. It felt like acid was burning in my chest and over-the-counter antacids like Tums did nothing for me. I used my health insurance to see a doctor to treat it. The visit was quick. She asked me questions about my symptoms then prescribed me a drug within 15 minutes. Her diagnosis was GERD or gastroesophageal reflux disease and her solution was to take a "proton pump inhibitor" which reduces the amount of acid produced by the glands in your stomach.

The instructions were to take the large pill every morning before I ate. I immediately felt nauseous, then got a terrible headache later. Not only did I have chest pains but now I could not work because I felt too sick to function. It was a mess. Is this what we pay doctors to do?

Experiment with chemicals to "see" if they work only to cause more problems. Without knowing an alternative at the time, I went back to the same doctor and she prescribed another brand of the same type of medicine with the same instructions. I took it once and it gave me the same symptoms along with a terrible stomach ache. So I listened to my body, I stopped taking the medication and was determined to find a more effective solution.

At the time, my late cousin, who was a doctor, was dating a pharmacist. His boyfriend recommended I try Beano, a natural digestive enzyme that helps digest foods that cause gas. I started taking Beano before every meal and I eliminated acidic foods from my diet like orange juice, tomatoes, alcohol and fried foods. Within a week, my symptoms were gone. After two weeks and eliminating problem foods, I stopped taking Beano and the symptoms never returned. Amazing! Once again, the power of natural remedies activated my own body's ability to heal itself.

The third time I had a health issue that I resolved through naturopathy, I was 30 and I had gone back to my acidic diet. One night for dinner, I was downing some fried food with a hard cider, drinking very little water. Then while at a nightclub, dancing with some friends, I got an excruciating sharp pain in my lower left back that shot all the way down to my left leg. I fell to the ground in pain and my friend helped me limp to my car. It was the most painful thing I had ever experienced.

I met Master Wang, a week earlier at a teahouse in San Francisco. I remember how clear his skin was, it was as though he was glowing. I told him I was a video producer and I learned he was a healer interested in marketing his business. Clearly a case of synchronicity, Master Wang calls me the next day after my episode at the club.

He wanted me to produce a video ad for his program called "Total Vitality" that promotes proper hydration and an alkaline diet for optimal health. Little did I know, he would change my life forever. Given my condition, when he asked to hire me for video services I asked if we could do a trade. I would produce his business video in exchange for him teaching me his program so I could heal my ailment, which I later learned was sciatica. Sciatica is when a nerve in the lower spine becomes inflamed and causes pain in the back, hips and legs.

Master Wang was an incredible healer. He was a physician like no other I had ever encountered. The entire experience being in his care versus having an HMO medical doctor in an institutionalized hospital experience was like night and day. In a hospital, everything is gray and cold with fluorescent lights. With an HMO, in my experience the doctor is impersonal and in a rush since they have to see on average 20 patients a day [Ref 13]. On average, a doctor spends 13-24 minutes with a patient, sometimes less than that [Ref 14].

When I had GERD, my doctor saw me for about 10 minutes, asking questions without any physical examination then prescribing a drug that caused more harm than good. Sadly, this may be the experience of many people. I want to share my experience with Master Wang and the wisdom he shared about how to care for our own health to live optimally.

When Master Wang invited me to his teahouse, everything was made of cherry wood and bamboo. I remember sunlight streaming through the window as I sat at his tea table where he ceremoniously poured me a fresh cup of pu-erh tea. Everything was a teaching moment. He explained that in addition to the stimulation of caffeine in the tea, it also had theanine which has a calming effect, giving it a balanced energy unlike coffee. It also encourages the bowels to move, to help with constipation, a big problem in the Western world where most of our foods are unnatural.

Master Wang's pu-erh tea originated from Yunnan in China where he is from. It's made from ancient trees and is uniquely alkalizing as opposed to commercial teas from young bushes that make them acidic. Why is this important? The ph level of our foods affects the ph of our bodies. He explains the more alkaline the body is, the less prone to inflammation—the starting point for most chronic diseases, cancer, bone loss and more [Ref 15].

More amazing benefits of adding drinking pu-erh tea to your daily ritual: alkalizing, anti-inflammatory, digestive aid, weight loss, diabetes management & prevention, cardiovascular wellness, anxiety reduction and more.

Master Wang's intention from the start was to offer me self-empowerment. He gave me tools to help restore balance to heal myself and not be dependent on him or any drug. This was a revelation to someone like me being raised in a Western medical system that seems to want to keep people ignorant and sick to make money.

When I sat down at his tea table, I was relaxed and the tea felt nourishing and healing. Immediately, Master Wang tuned into me. He looked at the quality of my skin which can indicate dehydration or a poor diet. He was looking at my irises which can reveal a host of illnesses. Then he took my hands and gently twisted each finger. He explained that each finger is connected to meridians or energetic passageways in the body and that the flexibility of each finger reflects the health of every internal organ.

After Master Wang inspected my finger flexibility, he then said my colon was blocked and my left kidney was inflamed. I saw his ancient wisdom and knowledge as he assessed the health of my organs. I was amazed. He went into his herbal jars, preparing a mixture of herbs to treat the ill organs he identified.

He told me to boil them and drink a gallon of hot tea each morning before noon. He asked me if I had ever seen a river's speed in the morning slow and easy versus faster in the afternoon. He explained the tilt of the earth at certain times of the day also affects the flow of water in our bodies. Due to this, mornings are the best time to hydrate the body when it is most absorbent.

His program "Total Vitality" calls for proper hydration, ideally room temperature spring water (the purest, but watch out for added fluoride, which is a neurotoxin) and an alkaline diet. Since water makes up over 75% of the body, proper hydration supports overall health and immunity. Aim for 3-4 liters a day.

For my cleanse, I was instructed to drink a gallon of hot herbal tea in the morning to drive out the toxins in my organs. After 3 to 4 days of this simple ritual, almost 10+ pounds of food came out of my body like soft-serve ice cream. I was amazed. Since I am a thin person, I couldn't believe all that food was lodged in my body and how the tea helped it come out with ease. The large intestine and small intestine are almost 30 feet in length. I imagined 30+ years of sludge: GMOs, wheat gluten, cheese and processed meats, coming out of my body during this much needed cleanse.

During the cleanse, Master Wang advised me to give up junk food, meat, wheat, rice and dairy. This was all the food I ate. He introduced me to whole foods like fruits, vegetables and whole grains like millet, quinoa and amaranth. He taught me that raw pumpkin seeds drive out parasites in our guts and how the "nightshade" family of vegetables can cause inflammation.

Nightshade vegetables like potatoes, tomatoes, eggplant and peppers, while they have health benefits, also contain a toxic alkaloid called alpha-solanine which can aggravate inflammatory conditions that already exist [Ref 20].

I realize not everybody has access to a Master Wang but there are many resources for holistic healers and medical doctors returning to the naturopathic roots of Hippocrates. Integrative or functional medicine looks at the patient as a whole and uses natural modalities to treat illnesses. I am a firm believer in doing your own research—that is what has led me on my path to self healing.

Since studying with Master Wang in my early 30s, I've completely cut out GMOs and fast food in my diet. I am now 44 and in the best health of my life. I still follow his protocol of hydration and alkalinity which has kept any inflammatory or digestive issues away. When I feel out of balance I return to these two key elements to reset my system. He taught me that the most important teacher is yourself. Paying attention to how foods make you feel is a part of the process. Completely healing from chronic illnesses requires more than taking a pill. It takes a shift in consciousness around what real health is and making lifestyle changes to support the desire to live and feel well.

Juicing and Fasting To Heal Chronic Illnesses

One of my favorite food documentaries is "Fat, Sick and Nearly Dead." It's about Joe Cross, a man in his 40s, who suffered from an autoimmune disease called chronic urticaria, which is like chronic hives. He took steroids to control the disease, but had a host of unwanted side effects. At his wits end and feeling unwell, he decided to take matters into his own hands.

He went on a 60-day juice and veggie fast to reclaim his health while under the supervision of a doctor and nutritionist. He traveled across the US to inspire other Americans to make lifestyle changes to increase wellness. By the end of the film, he lost 100 pounds and was completely off of all medications and his disease was in remission. Joe Cross has inspired many people to detox with juices, thanks to his film and program called Reboot with Joe [Ref 21].

In addition to detoxing, there is the powerful practice of fasting. Fasting dates back to ancient healers like Hippocrates who said, "To eat when you are sick, is to feed your illness" [Ref. 29]. Using food abstinence to treat multiple health issues is not new. Many religions and philosophies practice fasting as a means to purification including Buddhism, Christianity, Islam, Judaism, Taoism, Jainism and Hinduism.

When doing a water fast, the body will begin to break itself down or what is known as autophagy.

Autophagy of "self-eating" is a self-preservation mechanism through which the body can remove the dysfunctional cells and recycle parts of them toward cellular repair and cleaning [Ref. 31]. Autophagy can typically take 2-4 days of fasting to begin. Results of autophagy can include a decrease in blood sugar, insulin, inflammation, cholesterol, blood pressure and weight [Ref. 30]. Fasting can also result in an increase in brain function, growth hormone which is vital to growth, metabolism, weight loss and muscle strength [Ref. 30]. It can also delay aging and expand one's life, prevent cancer and make chemotherapy more effective in combating cancer [Ref. 30].

Fasting not only helps the body to reset, it also sharpens the mind, heightens the senses and increases self-awareness. There are many types of fasting depending on your intention: to lose weight, reverse illness or allergies, feel lighter and clearer, or for spiritual reasons. A great documentary called "Fasting," on Amazon Prime video, explores seven types of fasting: Time-Restricted Feeding, Intermittent and Prolonged Fasting, Long-Term Water Fasting, Religious Fasting, Eating Disorders, Improvising or Fasting Unsafely, Fasting Mimicking Diet and Juice Fasting. I will cover a few of these but I highly suggest watching the film and doing your own research if you are interested.

Another great documentary series on Netflix called "(Un)Well" has an episode called "Fasting," that showcases fasting centers around the world where many chronically ill people go to heal after Western medicine makes them sicker. One is the Tanglewood Wellness Center in Guanacaste, Costa Rica, which reports that people from over 115 countries come to heal their illnesses through water-only fasting. People reported reversing diabetes, high blood pressure, cancer, arthritis, multiple sclerosis, inflammatory conditions and much more by fasting.

In one case, a two year old born with a heart defect fasted for five days and was off his medication. At this center, there is no medical supervision which can be dangerous for people with serious conditions. Long periods of fasting can make one light-headed and prone to falling and getting hurt, so take caution when fasting for long periods of time. As with anything, do your research so you are aware of the risks.

For less intensive fasting, what works for me is intermittent fasting, juice fasting and eliminating certain foods that cause allergic reactions. Intermittent fasting is simply where you skip a meal to allow the body time to digest and reset before eating again. In America, we are accustomed to over-eating. Fasting can really help aid in improving digestion and giving us more energy. By eliminating certain foods like meat, wheat, dairy and processed foods for a few weeks, while drinking large amounts of hot cleansing herbal teas and eating only whole foods reset my whole digestive system. Juice fasting is also a great starting point to reset the body.

When doing a fast, cleanse or detox, you become more aware of what foods feel good and what don't. After I did my two-week cleanse with Master Wang, I tuned into how much wheat and dairy made me bloated and constipated. Now that I know I am lactose and gluten-intolerant, I stick to a mostly dairy and gluten free diet and opt for hard cider or wine instead of beer which contains wheat gluten. I also realized how cloudy my brain was when I ate wheat daily. Now I eat dairy or wheat occasionally as a treat. The point is moderation.

Many people turn to allergy tests to determine what foods or substances cause issues in their body like soy, wheat, dairy, nuts, seafood, red meat and so on. Once you know what foods agree with you (or not), then you can choose the best diet for yourself.

Gut Health, Digestion and Probiotics

"All disease begins in the gut," said Hippocrates, credited as the "Father of Modern Medicine," who was in fact a naturopath. 80% of your immune system is in the gut, and about 90% your body's serotonin is too. This means if your gut isn't healthy, then your immune system and hormones won't function, and you will get sick [Ref. 22].

Many people who have consumed a typical American diet can truly benefit from a detox or cleanse. Gut health is a huge factor in maintaining wellness. I also take probiotics, drink 3-4 liters of water a day and mostly plant-based foods to ensure proper digestion.

Probiotics are live microorganisms that improve and restore the gut microbiota which decline as we age. Eating foods regularly with naturally occurring probiotics can improve digestion, like kombucha, miso, kimchee, sauerkraut, yogurt (non dairy if lactose intolerant) and natural fibrous foods like prunes, nuts and fruits. Prebiotic foods also aid in restoring gut health like dandelion greens, apples, artichokes, asparagus, bananas, berries, green vegetables, legumes, onions and garlic.

There are also almost 100 million nerve endings in your gastrointestinal tract. This is known as the Enteric Nervous System (ENS) so your gut is in direct communication to your brain (Ref. 182). So when people say they have a gut feeling or when they experience something bad and feel sick to their stomach, it's because there is an actual second brain in that area of the body as well (Ref. 182). So our gut health can directly affect our emotions and our mood.

Consuming artificial foods and intaking pharmaceuticals can be damaging to the intestinal lining so it's important to offset this with eating whole, natural foods and foods that are rich in digestive enzymes or probiotics to maintain good gut health. I personally take 60 billion probiotics every day to help with the digestion of gluten and dairy foods since I am gluten and dairy intolerant. I find my digestion is best when I am hydrated and eat a diet with a majority of leafy greens, high fiber vegetables, fruits while keeping foods harder to digest to a minimum.

However, if your body is out of balance or if you are regularly constipated, it's key to do a detox with natural foods and completely eliminate those problem foods until your body is eliminating (bowel movements) regularly and with ease. A balanced diet, adequate sleep and exercise are all vital to maintaining a healthy gut and healthy mood.

Types of Diets, Superfoods and Adaptogens

There are many types of diets and reasons why people choose them. People generally choose diets based on body type, health needs or spiritual reasons.

Some types of diets are omnivore; one who eats everything, carnivore; a meat-based diet, vegetarian; a vegetable-based diet, vegan; a vegetable-based with no dairy or animal products, raw; only raw vegetables and fruits, macrobiotic; only cooked vegetables (no fried) and whole grains, ketogenic; healthy fats and proteins, no carbohydrates, typically for those needing to reduce their sugar or weight, paleo; primarily vegetables, fruits and lean meat, and an elimination diet; which is where you eliminate certain foods that may be causing you health issues like gluten, dairy, fried foods or red meat.

Personally, I eat a paleo diet because I find the most balance and energy with this diet. I tried to be vegetarian several times in my life. The first time I tried it my skin became sallow then the second time I tried it I lost a lot of weight. I even worked with a holistic healer once who confirmed that my constitution was not at its best as a vegetarian. I do maintain an alkaline base, so I eat a majority of fruits and vegetables while enjoying lean meats to keep my immunity system strong.

Macrobiotic diets have shown to help those healing from illnesses like cancer. I became aware of this when I frequented my favorite vegan Tibetan restaurant in the Bay area called "Shangri-La." The food was so whole and clean. I felt so energized and nourished after. Raw foods while healthy can be too harsh to process for impaired systems like those going through chemotherapy. In a macrobiotic diet, the vegetables are all cooked by steaming, boiling or baking (no frying), so it's easier for the body to digest and become more alkaline.

Studies have shown that having a plant-based diet like veganism, no meat, dairy or animal derived products, and vegetarianism, just fruits, veggies and some dairy and eggs, have been on the rise since the increasing awareness of the numerous benefits of eating an alkaline diet for increased health and wellness.

The harm of the overconsumption of meats like red meat and pork which tend to be higher in fat than fish or chicken can lead to an acidic constitution which can make one more prone to illness. However, animal protein also has a host of benefits. Again, moderation is key.

Having an alkaline pH in the body is the most stable and resistant to diseases. High acidity pH in the body which is associated with eating fatty meats, fried foods, processed foods and sugary foods, is more inclined to inflammatory issues. Inflammation is the starting point to most illnesses, so having a more alkaline diet is our best immunity defense to disease.

More people are also choosing plant based diets because of the cruel ways animals are being treated and how destructive these meat farms are to the health of the environment.

Herbalist healer, Dr. Sebi and others healers like Master Wang, all maintain and model the belief that herbs and a plant-based alkaline diet as a way to cure all disease. I know this to be true in my experience of healing the pain of sciatica through alkalizing my diet in just a few weeks. More and more people are understanding today, just how powerful food can cause disease but also be the cure as well.

Superfoods are amazing to include in your diet because they are like powerhouse foods. They are nutrient-dense foods that can accelerate healing in the body. The reason why dark, leafy green vegetables are healthy is because they contain many nutrients and chlorophyll which is photosynthesized sunlight that supports skin, blood health and more.

Two superfoods that contain chlorophyll but are packed with more nutrients are chlorella and spirulina. Both are forms of algae, containing B vitamins and trace minerals that improve metabolism, mental functions and help minimize heart disease and diabetes (Ref. 183).

Many foods we eat are nutrient dense superfoods like nuts, berries, dark, leafy greens, green tea, avocados, ginger, garlic, mushrooms, olive oil, fish, and more. But you can also research other not so common superfoods that can be tossed into your morning smoothie to give your body an extra boost like maca root, chia seeds, flax seeds, acai berries, turmeric, cacao, camu camu and more.

Adaptogens are found in particular foods and herbs that help to achieve balance or homeostasis in the body and generally create a sense of wellness. Some of the superfoods I mentioned are also considered adaptogenic like maca, mushrooms, turmeric and more.

These are simple foods you can add to your diet as food, drink or supplements to create more wellness in your body, improve mood, reduce stress, anti-inflammatory properties and more. Some adaptogens are lavender, holy basil, goji berry, lion's mane, licorice and more.

Adaptogens like superfoods can help activate the body's own healing properties and achieve an optimal state. So if you are dealing with a health issue you can research and select whole foods along with some adaptogens and superfoods you can add to your diet to help your body achieve balance and wellness.

Chapter 2: Reflections:
What ways can you integrate more natural foods and hydration to your current diet to feel and live better?

Chapter 3

Cannabis Cures: Our Misunderstood Cousin

Cannabis, also known as reefer, pot, weed, hashish, dope, ganja, bud and grapes, is by far my favorite plant medicine. The first time I smoked weed, I was 15 years old. My older cousin made a homemade three-foot-tall bong from a PVC pipe. I took a big hit and let out a big cough. I remember chillin' on a sofa in my cousin's room, with blacklight posters glowing with "Sweet Potato Pie" by Outkast playing.

I felt giddy and my senses were heightened. I could really hear the highs in the song so clearly. The artwork seemed to vibrate. I felt like I had dialed into a magical universe. Ever since that day, I have been a user of the plant recreationally, spiritually and for medicinal cures to help alleviate insomnia, depression, anxiety and more.

Historical Benefits of Cannabis

It is my belief that throughout history, powerful people or things are vilified at some point. This includes natural cures being discredited in the early 1900s by the Flexner Report [Ref. 36].

Perhaps this vilification is out of fear of the plant's power or the desire to control its influence and impact.

Either way, cannabis is one of the most misunderstood plants today. It has a complicated history, particularly in the United States.

Both hemp and marijuana come from the cannabis plant. There are over 50,000 documented uses of the hemp plant [Ref. 34]. Hemp, the more fibrous part of the plant stalk, is used to make countless items like clothes, rope, paper, wood, bioplastics and more. Hemp seeds are high in nutrition and a great source of protein, omega-3, omega-6, vitamin E and minerals, such as phosphorus, potassium, sodium, magnesium, sulfur, calcium, iron and zinc [Ref. 33].

Before marijuana was criminalized in 1937, it was a federal law for landowners to grow hemp. This law passed in Virginia in 1619 and even the founding father, George Washington grew hemp. At that time, hemp was considered legal tender and was used like money in Pennsylvania, Virginia, and Maryland [ref. 53]. By the 1800s, cotton became more popular than hemp. But when hemp became known for its medicinal properties, it became a problem.

Beginning in the 1830s, Anglo-Americans and Europeans discovered the medicinal benefits of cannabis. Sir William Brooke O'Shaughnessy, an Irish doctor studying in India, documented that cannabis reduced digestive symptoms of cholera, a deadly bacteria found in contaminated water and food, that caused a global pandemic in the 1800's. By the late 19th century, cannabis extracts could be bought in pharmacies and doctors' offices in America and Europe to help with stomach aches, migraines, inflammation, insomnia and other health issues [Ref. 42].

Cannabis Used as an Etheogen

Aside from cannabis' practical, medicinal and recreational uses, it's also considered a sacred plant in many cultures. It is an entheogen or a sacred plant that is used ceremonially to alter perception or consciousness for spiritual growth and healing. Many ancient cultures around the world have used cannabis in this way.

The sacred use of cannabis goes back 2,700 years ago to ancient China where it was found in the remains of a mummy who was "well dressed and clearly respected, perhaps a shaman, his grave held interesting items, including a bow, harp, and even 789 grams of marijuana" [Ref. 45.] We assume he used the sacred herb for shamanistic rituals and divination or the practice of seeking knowledge of the future by channeling a spiritual dimension.

In China, around the 4th century, Taoist texts cite the use of cannabis burned in "ritual incense burners." Ge Hong, a Taoist practitioner, philosopher, physician and writer during the Eastern Jin dynasty, says "For those who begin practicing the Tao it is not necessary to go into the mountains...Some with purifying incense and sprinkling and sweeping are also able to call down the Perfected Immortals."

Also in 5th century China, the Mingyi bielu or the "Supplementary Records of Famous Physicians", written by the Taoist pharmacologist Tao Hongjing, says that "Hemp-seeds are very little used in medicine, but the magician-technicians say that if one consumes them with ginseng it will give one preternatural knowledge of events in the future" [Ref. 44].

In India, the sacred Hindu text "Atharvaveda," which was written sometime around 2000–1400 BCE, mentions cannabis as one of the "five sacred plants...which release us from anxiety" and "that a guardian angel resides in its leaves." [Ref. 44]. The Indian Hindu sacred scripture, the Vedas also refer to it as a "source of happiness, joy-giver, liberator" and "the gods sent hemp to the human race so that they might attain delight, lose fear and have sexual desires" [Ref. 44].

In India, cannabis use has been around for thousands of years. Shiva is the god commonly linked to cannabis. Within Hinduism, there is a sect of mystical holy men called, Sadhus, who have "relinquished themselves of [the earthly life] of modern conveniences, and they perform religious acts or blessings for the aid of others" [Ref. 46]. Sadhus use cannabis in religious ceremonies and holy festivities. They consume it by smoking it and sometimes a special drink called 'Bhang' [Ref. 46].

In 1930, Rastafarianism began in Jamaica following the coronation of Ethiopian Emperor Haile Selassie I [Ref. 47]. They consider smoking cannabis or "ganja" as "wisdom weed" helping one gain wisdom and a deeper connection to one's "inner spiritual self, Jah (God) and Creation" [Ref. 51].

While it is unclear, when Rastafarians first considered cannabis to be a sacred plant, by the late 1940s ganja smoking was practiced at the Rastafarian community by the pioneering preacher; Leonard Howell who is considered the first Rastafarian [Ref. 44]. Perhaps the most influential Rastafarian is Bob Marley, whose persona and music attracted global attention to Rastafarian beliefs and the smoking of ganja for generations to come [Ref. 47].

Why It Works: Our Misunderstood Cousin

First, let's understand why it works. Cannabis contains at least 113 distinct cannabinoids, which are also found in other plants like licorice and echinacea [Ref. 38]. The human body has cannabinoid receptors and its own Endocannabinoid System (ECS) which regulates many functions of the human body. The ECS affects neural functions of the body, "including the control of movement and motor coordination, learning and memory, emotion and motivation, addictive-like behavior and pain modulation" [Ref. 38].

The body naturally produces endocannabinoids which are present in various organs and tissues, such as the muscles, brain and circulating cells. Endocannabinoids become active when they bind with a cannabinoid receptor [Ref. 35]. So simply, humans contain the same compounds to that of cannabis and all plants for that matter which is why their healing properties work. We are in fact related.

Cannabis can be smoked, eaten in food or as a drink or applied topically to receive its therapeutic effects. Cannabidiol oil or CBD is used for its medicinal properties without the psychoactive element of THC. Used for reducing inflammation and pain relief due to arthritis, multiple sclerosis, surgery, chemotherapy and more, CBD is a natural and safer pain reliever than opioids, NSAIDS and other chemicals that cause undesirable side effects and in some cases, death.

CBD also helps with mental health issues like anxiety, depression, insomnia, post-traumatic stress disorder, epilepsy and more without the serious side effects of pharmaceuticals. It has also shown success in treating health issues in babies, the elderly and pets.

Marijuana or the psychoactive part of cannabis is found in the flowering parts and leaves of only the female plant. This is why I think this plant has a feminine, goddess energy to it. This is the part of the plant containing THC, or delta-9-tetrahydrocannabinol, which has the psychoactive compound that makes people "high."

THC activates dopamine in the brain which affects mood and pleasure. THC is perhaps my favorite part of cannabis. THC can make one feel euphoria, relaxation, laughter, heightened sensory perception and an increased appetite aka "the munchies."

But THC can also make some people feel paranoid and anxious. I find this to be true at times but it passes and the benefits outweigh the temporary discomfort. Research suggests it's because certain compounds, including THC, bind to endocannabinoid receptors in various parts of your brain, including the amygdala, which regulates your response to fear like paranoia, anxiety and stress.

When you use cannabis with high levels of THC, your brain suddenly receives an excess of cannabinoids more than usual. This excess of cannabinoids may overstimulate the amygdala, making you feel anxiety and fear.

Some tips to combat this issue: if you still want to consume it, is to consume less or be sure you are in a relaxing setting. What's fascinating about cannabis is that it contains both THC and CBD to regulate each other. The ratio of each can vary but if you tend toward paranoia and anxiety a higher CBD content will ease the psychoactive component. For some people, just using CBD for its therapeutic effects is enough. I find this to be the case when I use CBD to help me relax or sleep.

In recent years, I discovered a company called "Foria" as in euphoria, that's created a coconut oil based spray with THC, CBD and an herbal version, used to increase sexual pleasure. They are advocates of self-pleasure, or masturbation, encouraging more self-understanding of our own bodies. They are interested in making sex, more enjoyable, particularly for women. I have used Foria for years and I must say the results are astounding. I highly recommend this product.

Debunking The Myth: The Vilification and Racializing of Marijuana

Despite the therapeutic effects of cannabis, it's important to understand why there is a negative stigma around its use to this day. Up until the 19th century, cannabis and hemp were legally consumed for medicinal and practical purposes in the United States. It was never considered a hard drug like opium and heroin, which were prohibited under the Harrison Narcotics Act of 1914.

However by the 1930s, cannabis was coined as "The Gateway Drug," or its use could lead to using harsher drugs like cocaine and heroin, by Harry Anslinger, the first commissioner of the Federal Bureau of Narcotics (later known as the DEA, Drug Enforcement Administration). He campaigned against cannabis after his attack on alcohol which was illegal from 1920-1933 [Ref. 40].

Anslinger was an early architect of the "War on Drugs" where he pushed for "harsh drug penalties and focused on demonizing racial and immigrant groups [like Latinos and Blacks], including jazz musicians like Billie Holiday" [Ref. 121]. Interestingly, prior to his position as commissioner, he stated that marijuana was mild and claiming that it drove people mad was "absurd fallacy" [Ref. 113]. But once appointed, he changed his position and held office for an unprecedented 32 years until 1962 [Ref. 121].

Ansliger created "The Gore Files," "so-called reports that" spread propaganda through broadcast and print media, claiming that cannabis led people to "commit criminal acts and violence" [Ref. 112]. His government "mass hysteria campaign" with the US federal government called marijuana 'The Assassin of Youth,' claiming that it was turning "sane young men into hideous criminal beasts, sex fiends; the worst kind of cold blooded murderers" [Ref. 113].

Prior to the Mexican Revolution in 1910, this time period, the plant was referred to as cannabis. But renaming the plant as "marijuana" in the U.S. at this time underscored the drug's "Mexican-ness" and fueled anti-immigrant fear [Ref. 40].

In 1994, investigative journalist Eric Schlosser wrote for *The Atlantic*, "The prejudices and fears that greeted these peasant immigrants also extended to their traditional means of intoxication: smoking marijuana. Police officers in Texas claimed that marijuana incited violent crimes, aroused a 'lust for blood,' and gave its users 'superhuman strength.' Rumors spread that Mexicans were distributing this 'killer weed' to unsuspecting American schoolchildren" [Ref. 42].

One New York Times headline from 1925 says "Mexican, Crazed by Marihuana, Runs Amuck with Butcher Knife." These are just some examples of what led to the criminalization of "marijuana" that causes disproportionately more Latinos and Blacks to be imprisoned for cannabis related crimes, in contrast to white Americans [Ref. 53].

Despite there being no scientific evidence of any of these claims, 29 states outlawed marijuana between 1916-1931. In 1936, the film "Reefer Madness" created waves of fear for years to come alarming "parents [to think] that drug dealers would invite their teenagers to jazz parties and get them hooked on 'reefer'." A year later, President Roosevelt would sign the Marihuana Tax Act of 1937 which banned marijuana across the United States [Ref. 42].

Research has shown alcohol to be more dangerous than marijuana. According to the U.S. Drug Enforcement Administration's fact sheet on the plant says that "No death from overdose of marijuana has been reported" [Ref. 42].

Just a year after the Marijuana Tax Act passed, New York Mayor, Fiorello LaGuardia created the "LaGuardia Report" as he was skeptical of the law. He assembled a committee, made up of the scientists and doctors, who spent five years researching and investigating marijuana use and its effects [Ref. 48]. The LaGuardia Committee published the report in 1944 stating that pot was harmless, did not lead to crimes or addiction, and was actually quite therapeutic.

Criminalization and Legalization of Cannabis

No one has ever died of a marijuana overdose. So why was it classified as a hard drug like heroin and coined the "gateway drug" to harder drugs for so long?

In my opinion, it was a way to control culture. Cannabis, like all entheogens (psychoactive plant medicines), expand the mind so people are more liberated. I think the culture of legalization started to change once the government understood they could monetize it. But cannabis use is safer than legal alcohol, tobacco and pharmaceuticals that can lead to death

The U.S. Marijuana Tax Act of 1937 prohibited marijuana use, but allowed medical use in some cases. Then in 1970, the Controlled Substances Act classified cannabis as a Schedule I drug, like heroin, which prohibited its use of any kind.

At this time, some states moved toward decriminalization, so offenders were not prosecuted for small amounts. By the 1990s, some states began to legalize medical marijuana. By 2012, Washington and Colorado were the first states to legalize recreational use of cannabis (Ref. 179).

Medical use of cannabis is now legal in 40 states including Washington, DC and recreational use is also legal in 21 states (Ref. 179).

CBD made from the plant's flowers legalized by the Agriculture Improvement Act of 2018, allowing it to be farmed and sold in all 50 states in the U.S. Legal CBD must have a THC content level of less of .3%

CBD has proven to help heal numerous health issues, including alleviating depression, anxiety and insomnia. It reduces pain, blood pressure, psychotic symptoms and can help prevent diabetes, cancer, Alzheimer's disease and many other illnesses, without the serious side effects of man-made drugs [Ref. 32].

With the racialized history of people of color being disproportionately criminalized for cannabis use and possession, I need to acknowledge the detainment of WNBA basketball star Brittney Griner in Russia and how I feel that she was profiled for her race, gender and sexuality.

In February 2022, Griner was detained at a Russian airport, accused of possessing vape cartridges containing THC which is illegal in Russia. A week later, Russia invaded Ukraine, with airstrikes at multiple sites. With the timing of this invasion, U.S. President Biden's anti-Russian sentiments, then over five months later, she plead guilty even though it was a mistake since it's legal in the U.S. She was sentenced to nine years of imprisonment (Ref. 180).

After being wrongfully detained for over 8 months, Griner was released in exchange for the release of Russian weapons trader Victor Bout, known as the "merchant of death" who was in U.S. custody for over ten years (Ref. 184). It is inferred that Griner was caught in a "geopolitical conflict" between the U.S. and Russia (Ref. 184).

The Popularity of Cannabis: Then and Now

Throughout history, the biggest advocates of cannabis use have been artists. I believe their advocacy is in part why cannabis is legal in almost all of the U.S.

It's no secret that THC is a psychoactive substance so it naturally makes your creative juices flow, which is why I love to smoke and get creative.

Cannabis use was a big influence on Black creativity with jazz musicians in the Jazz Era of the 1920s-1930s. Louis Armstrong's song, "Muggles" is what jazz musicians called marijuana at the time (Ref. 185). Cab Calloway performed many songs in honor of the psychoactive plant, one called "Reefer Man" (Ref. 185). Other potheads of the time were Charlie Parker, Billie Holiday, Thelonius Monk and Bessie Smith (Ref. 186).

Marijuana also sparked creativity for artists during the hippie movement of the 1960s-1970s. These included Janis Joplin, the Doors, the Grateful Dead, and Bob Dylan who introduced the Beatles to weed in 1964 (Ref. 187).

Along with fellow Rastafarian reggae artist Bob Marley, Peter Tosh was also a smoker and advocate of the plant with his hit song "Legalize It" (Ref. 187). Bob Marley refers to smoking ganga in songs including "Kaya," the album title track from 1978, which is another name for cannabis. Reggae music influenced cannabis use in many bands like the Clash, the Police, and UB40 (Ref. 187). In 1978, Rick James released his hit "Mary Jane" becoming an anthem for potheads everywhere.

In the 1980s, the punk music and skater scene in Venice Beach, California, was anti-establishment and smoking cannabis was an expression of this. Skating started to merge with hip-hop at this time as well, seen later in the 2000s with hip-hop artists like Lupe Fiasco's song "Kick, Push" and Pharrell's nickname being "Skateboard P."

The Beastie Boys is a perfect example of a band that started hard-core punk, then crossed over into hip-hop and rap. They wrote many songs with lyrics about smoking cannabis like "What Comes Around" and "SO WHAT'CHA WANT."

By the 1990s, smoking weed became more acceptable with artists like Dr. Dre, Snoop Dogg, and Cypress Hill, having songs, if not entire albums, dedicated to the plant. Most notably "The Chronic," Dr. Dre's debut album featuring Snoop Dogg.

Many films over the years popularized cannabis smoking with the classic "Cheech and Chong" series, "Dazed and Confused," "Half-Baked," "How High," "Friday," and " Harold and Kumar Go To White Castle."

Today, with cannabis legalization on the rise, smoking weed is more acceptable, and a safer form of recreation than alcohol. It is commonplace for people to know the difference between indica and sativa now—the first is relaxing and the other more energizing. As in ancient times, cannabis was used for healing, spirituality, recreation and creativity. It's still creating a safe outlet for people to enjoy themselves today.

<u>Chapter 3: Reflections</u>:
What ways can cannabis enhance your wellness?

Chapter 4

Entheogens: Expanding the Gateway to Our Consciousness

First off, I don't want to glorify the use of psychoactive medicines like mushrooms or ayahuasca and say that they are for everybody. It takes courage to face the realities these substances can show you, and a commitment to work on yourself and integrate your new insights into your journey.

At times, unwanted side effects can come before you get to the real magic of these plant medicines, but they do pass. I can only speak from my own experience and say that if you are curious about expanding the limits of your mind or going deeper into healing emotional or mental trauma, this is a viable, effective option.

Always do your own research, know there is risk but the pay off can change your life for the better. This is my personal insight and research into how these substances when done responsibly can deepen your journey into healing and self-realization.

Psychedelics are still illegal in most parts of the world and have been long vilified. But "as compared to opioids, alcohol and tobacco, psychedelics have low addictive potential and benign toxicity" according to Frontiers in Media, one of the most cited science journals in the world, founded by
Henry Markram and Kamila Markram, two Swiss neuroscientists [Ref. 62].

While I see the value in using these substances intentionally for self-exploration, self-development and healing, I am by no means condoning the abuse of these drugs. They can have a destructive effect on people's lives if not used wisely. Again, please do your own research and use caution and moderation.

My intention is to reveal the truth behind why these psychoactive medicines have been revered by ancient indigenous healers, modern day scientists and doctors for their healing powers. I think wanting to "trip" when you're young is natural in any culture especially if you are creative or spiritually-inclined. To want to explore the limits of your mind through psychedelics can be an expansive and revelatory experience.

Historically, through the use of plant medicines, indigenous people created bridges to the divine."Shamans are intermediaries or messengers between the human world and the spirit worlds. Shamans are said to treat ailments and illnesses by mending the soul" [Ref. 76]. The earliest account of entheogens or psychedelics was the use of peyote in Mexico dating back to 5,700 years ago [Ref. 123].

Traditionally used ceremonially by indigenous cultures for religious or shamanic healing purposes, the word "entheogen" is the term I like to use to describe these unique psychoactive medicines. "En-Theo" means "full of God" or "becoming the divine within," so that once the entheogen is ingested, one has a visionary and sensory experience with the divine.

Dr. Humphry Osmond, a believer and user of psychoactive substances, was the psychiatrist who coined the word "psychedelic" which means "mind manifesting." Ahead of his time, he used mescaline and later LSD as a therapy to treat mental illness in his patients. He introduced mescaline to Aldous Huxley, the author of "Doors of Perception." Huxley's personal account of the transformation he undergoes while taking a psychedelic is one of my favorite books. I recommend reading it if you are curious.

I still recall my first puff of cannabis sending me into a blissful, expansive state. To this day, it still brings me peace, comfort or a jolt of creative energy. Most psychedelics that have a psychoactive effect are typically used for recreational purposes to "trip out," and just have fun.

Psychonauts are people who use plant medicines to expand their consciousness. The use of plant medicines for spiritual purposes has roots in tribal ceremonies and shamanism. In recent years, it is more commonplace for people to seek such healing in a safe, controlled setting like how it was done traditionally.

What makes using entheogens different from psychedelics our intention and the container in which we do the psychoactive substance. When I used psychedelics recreationally, I still had a profound spiritual experience that brought greater self-awareness, overall well-being and personal development.

After cannabis, I tried various entheogens like psilocybin or magic mushrooms, San Pedro, ayahuasca, LSD and MDMA. With each, I had a transcendental experience that would change me forever. These experiences made me more open and aware of my value and my power to create the life I want. But everyone is different and will have a unique experience.

Bear in mind, entheogens are not suitable for everyone. They can have adverse effects, if you are taking SSRI (Selective serotonin reuptake inhibitor) or MAIO (Monoamine Oxidase Inhibitors) drugs, so please consult your physician if you are considering consuming entheogens.

The Entheogenic Medicine: Reunion with the Source

What is profound to me is how my entheogenic experiences healed some unresolved trauma I felt inside. The medicine healed an emotional wound causing me to suffer that I wasn't even aware was an issue. This is why it's been effective for people struggling to transform unresolved trauma underneath their addictive behaviors.

When taking the plant medicines in a safe, natural environment, the trees and natural environment speak to me without words in an unspoken connection. On my journeys, Mother Earth lets me know that I am a part of her and she is in me. We are one. There is no separation, only love and connection.

This is also known as "ego dissolution" or "ego death" which is key in transforming the mind. Ego dissolution according to Stanislav Grof, one of the pioneers of research on altered consciousness is "an ecstatic state, characterized by the loss of boundaries between the subject and the objective world, with ensuing feelings of unity with other people, nature, the entire Universe, and God" [Ref. 61].

This love and unity from the plants communicated to me each time mystically healed parts of me I didn't even know were wounded. That is the wisdom and power of Mother Earth. The power of plant medicines heal the wound of fear and separation we inherit from society and our relationships to welcome us back into our original state where the inherent connection between humans, Earth and the cosmos is unsevered. The expansion of consciousness back to this truth can leave one's life changed forever.

The power of the Earth and her plants go back to 4.5 billion years. Modern humans go back to only about 200,000 years. This difference is a testament to the Earth's knowledge and power and a reminder that no matter what humans do to the Earth, the Earth will continue with or without us. Sit with that truth. How fortunate are we to have access to her infinite wisdom and knowledge?

Precautions for a Good Trip: Set and Setting

First a bit of self-care, before doing any entheogen, make sure you are rested, hydrated, eaten at least a small meal and are in a mentally stable place. If these basic needs are not met, you may have a bad trip. I also advise you not to take more than one entheogen at a time and not to mix with alcohol or pharmaceuticals.

There have been numerous cases of fentanyl-laced street drugs like MDMA and non-entheogenic drugs like cocaine, heroin and others. Fentanyl is a lethal opioid that has killed many users in recent years. Fentanyl test strips are available for purchase at dancesafe.org, bunkpolice.com, and even amazon.com or at your local health department or community organization to ensure what you are taking is not laced with this deadly substance [Ref. 79].

Bad trips can happen for various reasons and in some cases it's not necessarily a bad thing. According to Sting, in a recent Netflix documentary, "Have a Good Trip: Adventures in Psychedelics," he says that bad trips are just what you need sometimes to "kick your ego's ass and be taken down a notch." [Ref. 63] I think there is a lesson in every trip, good or bad, that holds some wisdom and a lesson to be learned. Whatever the case, you are likely to experience a transformation.

To ensure a good trip on entheogens, there are a number of factors to consider. First is where did the medicine come from, and is it pure or tainted? The energy behind who cultivated it and how, can influence how it will affect you. Then there are the factors of "set and setting" [Ref. 54]. Set refers to your mindset when you take the medicine. Are you feeling positive and grounded or in a negative state and ungrounded? In my experience, the medicine amplifies the state you are already in, so it's important to be in a clear, positive space before you ingest it.

Setting is also key to the quality of your experience. My recommendation is to take the medicines in the solitude of nature so that your mind and spirit are free to soar and not fall into paranoia of what others are thinking, let alone the police. Also, listening to or creating music you enjoy is a great enhancement to any medicine journey you take.

Today I am more interested in using entheogens so I can journey deeper into the divine, into myself and have a profound experience that will leave me feeling healed, more whole and achieve a deeper sense of who I am and what I am here to do.

The Effects of Entheogens

Entheogens directly affect and mimic serotonin, a neurotransmitter that sends messages between the brain and the body. Serotonin enhances feelings of happiness, focus and calmness, and is responsible for regulating "mood, sleep, digestion, nausea, wound healing, bone health, blood clotting and sexual desire" [Ref. 70].

The term "trust your gut feeling" is actually confirmed to be true by science since "about 100 million nerve cells line the gastrointestinal tract, making up the Enteric Nervous System (ENS)" [Ref. 72]. The ENS in the gut communicates with the brain, sending neurochemicals like dopamine and serotonin, the "happy hormones," that affect mood and mental health [Ref. 70]. Over 90% of these chemicals along with other major neurotransmitters that affect mood can be found in the gut which is why gut health is connected to mental health [Ref. 72].

The use of entheogens increases the neuroplasticity of the brain to learn new ways of thinking and responding to stimuli or situations [Ref. 59]. This is important because as toddlers, our brains have about "15,000 synapses per neuron"[Ref. 73]. But by the time we are adults, we can have about half that amount of synapses which is communication between neurons. Neurons are cells responsible for our senses, the ability to move and a host of brain and body functions [Ref. 73].

An increase of neuroplasticity not only increases your learning and cognitive capabilities but also helps in "recovery from traumatic brain injuries, strengthening areas where function is lost or has declined" [Ref. 73]. Entheogens can be healing for those who have experienced psychological trauma or wanting to transform addiction and are seeking ways to heal emotionally.

As with any drug, there can be side effects or adverse reactions so please use your own discretion. I only speak from my own experiences and hope to inspire others to find their own way. I believe that entheogens can cause revelatory experiences that connect you more deeply to yourself, your purpose and your destiny.

I also find that these plant medicines can open your creative valve so inspiration flows more easily. I have also gained a greater self-awareness of my worth and personal power which are crucial elements to fulfilling one's life's purpose.

On ayahuasca, I have had visions of key moments in my life–of my past, present and future– that transformed who I am and guided my course by revealing my purpose to me.

The Multi-Dimensional Experience of Entheogens

I have experienced ESP or the extra-sensory perception throughout my life. I have seen and felt people's aura (the energy surrounding them) or vibration which tells me if this person is safe for me or not. Sometimes I see points of light that sparkle in bright colors like purple, red, gold or silver. These stars twinkle at me, when I have a brilliant thought, profound realization or when someone makes a truthful statement in a conversation.

To me, it's just the universe speaking to me. It speaks to all of us. The question is are we aware and paying attention to the signs? The plants open your inner eye.

Entheogens simply open your perception to things that are already there, you just may not be open to the messages. The visionary experiences I have had are many. Once I was doing mushrooms in the desert, which to me is one of the best places to do entheogens.

There, you are free of walls to inhibit your astral travel and EMF radiation that you would find in large cities.

In the desert, for a moment I saw energetic lines of light that connected everything. To me, it was the World Wide Web and not the internet, although that is what it's based on, but the actual web of life that interconnects us all. You can see proof that it exists when you travel across the planet and run into someone you know. This is not a coincidence, it's a synchronicity or reflection of this divine web we are all linked to that is ever present and working in our lives.

Renowned psychologist Carl Jung refers to this as the "collective unconscious," or the idea that we are all connected with our own unique personality. I call it God, the universe or great spirit. When you recognize the innate intelligence of the universe and your thoughts, words and actions are in alignment, then the universe will bring you exactly what you desire. Synchronicity is manifestation at work.

One mystical experience I had of synchronicity was when I was touring as a videographer for the Goddess Alchemy Project, a spiritual hip-hop group. Their philosophy and lyrics incorporated themes of spirituality like sacred geometry, numerology and mysticism. We were on tour in Maui and had an amazing entheogenic experience.

We first paid respect to Pele, the Hawaiian volcanic goddess, by offering her tobacco and whiskey. We then took some mushroom chocolates and took a long hike through this amazing private land, rich with flora and fauna. By the time the medicine started to work we reached a lagoon with a waterfall. We all grounded out in this magical place for the moment; some went for a swim, others danced, laughed or hugged it out.

It was at this time I began having inner visions of this vibrational image I had never seen before. Later, I would come to know it as the sacred geometric shape called a "Sri Yantra," which is a mystical diagram of interlocking triangles that represents the connection between the cosmos and the human body.

Sacred geometry is rooted in the idea that God created the universe with a geometric plan that many mathematicians like Plato, Kepler and other cultures, have recognized as recurring mystical patterns.

Later, I traveled with the Goddess Alchemy Project to Big Island Hawaii. There we stayed at the Sri Yantra palace. The property had the divine design everywhere, on the entrance, windows and walls just like I had seen in my vision. This synchronicity was another example of how we are all connected to a higher consciousness working on our behalf. Synchronicity gives me comfort, knowing that I am being supported in following my purpose and passion.

Visionary Psychonauts Birthing New Worlds

Not many people know this, but some of the greatest thinkers of our times used entheogens to manifest their grand visions. Steve Jobs, founder of Apple, admitted to having taken LSD up to 15 times between 1972-1974, [Ref. 56]. Jobs said that "LSD was a positive life-changing experience for me," and that he used it to spark his creative imagination [Ref. 56]. Since Jobs started Apple in 1976 just two years later, it has been suggested that his inspiration for his groundbreaking company, Apple, came from one of these acid (LSD) trips [Ref. 57].

Bill Wilson, the founder of Alcoholics Anonymous, a program that has helped countless people overcome addiction to alcohol, shared that his ability to heal his alcohol addiction was the result of a spiritual experience he had on an LSD trip [Ref. 55].

British author and polymath Gerald Heard was a psychedelic pioneer who tried LSD for the first time in the mid-1950s, as a catalyst for spiritual insight. "There are the colors and the beauties, the designs, the beautiful way things appear," Heard shared in an interview. "But that's only the beginning. Suddenly you notice that there aren't these separations" [Ref. 58]. By separation, he meant between people and suddenly the entheogens help you experience true empathy.

Through his work, he opened the door for fellow psychonaut luminaries like Aldous Huxley and Timothy Leary to follow his lead.

Aldous Huxley, British author and philosopher, known for his celebrated yet controversial novel "Brave New World," was also a user of psychedelics. He stated that psychedelics helped people see the world, "as is" with a "mind at large" or what I like to call a bird's eye view. Bird's eye view to me is the point of meditation where one can see everything is related to each other with purpose and meaning. The result is an increased awareness of our connection to ourselves, others, the spirit world and the Earth. This is the power of entheogens.

Non-Psychoactive Therapies and Substances

Before I go into various entheogens, I want to acknowledge those who may not be able to do psychedelics or may not want to but still experience a heightened state and achieve a therapeutic effect that increases dopamine. This is a list of various activities or substances that can create a similar effect without "tripping" or having hallucinogenic visions.

- Breathwork, Chanting and Meditation
- Exercise, Dancing and Yoga

- Sunlight
- Fasting
- Ice Baths
- Sound Healing
- Microdosing Psychedelics
- Cacao
- Temazcal and Saunas
- Tantra and Orgasms

This is just a short list to explore but I encourage you to do your own research and see what works for you in creating more wellness in your life.

Types of Entheogens, Their Effects and a Brief History

While there are many entheogenic plant medicines and substances, I will only discuss some I have experience with. These substances have been used throughout history in ancient to modern times, either recreationally or with a spiritual intention. The effects are the same in that they affect your serotonin receptors and increase neuroplasticity. Serotonin, considered the "happy hormone," makes you feel good. Neuroplasticity increases synaptic activity in the brain, making it easier to unlearn and relearn new behavioral patterns such as transforming addiction to unhealthy substances or to toxic behavioral patterns or into healthier behaviors. In part, why these substances can be transformational and life-changing.

Psilocybin aka Magic Mushrooms

Psilocybin is the active substance found in magic mushrooms that causes altered moods, perception, visions and sensations in users. Historically, indigenous cultures in pre-Columbian Mesoamerica—now, southern North America and most of Central America—used these mushrooms along with other entheogens for "magical, therapeutic and religious purposes" [Ref. 67]. The Aztec, Maya, Zapotec and Olmec people used these powerful entheogens during healing rituals and religious ceremonies to communicate with the divine or astral realm, causing altered states of consciousness [Ref. 67].

Today more people, even in the medical world, are looking to entheogens to heal trauma and many forms of mental illness and emotional dis-ease. These substances were long looked at as suspect but that is all changing because the effective results are undeniable. A recent study by Columbia University treated over 200 patients with psilocybin aka "magic mushrooms" for depression were relieved for up to 12 weeks with a single 25mg dose of psilocybin [Ref. 60]. The majority of people who had the highest dose reported feeling a sharp decline in depression and it was more effective for them than man-made medications.

Recently, the Food and Drug Administration has cited psilocybin and MDMA as "breakthrough therapies," for treatment of mental illnesses like depression, PTSD and autism on their way to being approved under strict supervision by 2023 [Ref. 59].

María Sabina, born around 1894, was a famous priestess, curandera (shaman) and oral poet called "La Señora" from Sierra Mazateca, in Oaxaca, Mexico where certain mushrooms are considered sacred. She held sacred healing ceremonies, known as veladas, that provided the "intake of psilocybin mushrooms, Mazatec chants, tobacco smoke, mezcal consumption, and ointments extracted from medicinal plants" in a safe, sacred container [Ref. 66]. She was one of the first curanderas to open her ceremonies to foreigners and teach them about the uses and effects of magic mushrooms.

In the early 1950's, one foreigner who would come to participate in her Mazatec mushroom rituals, was Robert Gordon Wasson, an American banker, ethnomycologist and writer, along with his wife. The ritual was for finding missing people and important objects. Wasson told her that he had been looking for his son, which was not true [Ref. 68]. He took a picture of her saying he would keep it confidential. Then shortly after, Wasson published his experience with María Sabina, including her photo and disclosing her location, called "Seeking the Magic Mushroom," in an issue of LIFE magazine in June 1957. The publication immediately went viral [Ref. 66, 68].

The article raised curiosity about these magic mushroom rituals in people around the world, especially beatniks and hippies [Ref. 68]. By the 1960s, some famous visitors that came to see Sabina were John Lennon, Aldous Huxley, Walt Disney and Carlos Castaneda [Ref. 69].

Gasson would profit immensely from his publication and the knowledge he gained from Sabina without facing any consequences for deceiving her. Because his actions caused an influx of foreigners seeking out her rituals, her community ostracized her and burned down her house. The Mexican police became aware of her popularity and believed she had been selling mushrooms to foreigners, which was illegal and she was briefly jailed, ultimately dying in poverty [Ref. 68].

While it is not commonly known, since the 1960s, academic institutions and the pharmaceutical industry have been doing research on the use of psilocybin as a treatment for mental health issues. Dr. Timothy Leary, an American psychologist, psychedelic advocate and writer, along with Richard Alpert, the fellow psychologist, writer and yoga guru later known as Ram Dass, first led experimental studies with psilocybin during this time called the "Harvard Psilocybin Project" at Harvard University [Ref. 65].

Their Concord Prison Experiment was one of the first studies conducted which involved "the administration of psilocybin-assisted group psychotherapy to 32 prisoners in an effort to reduce recidivism (or likelihood to commit a crime again) rates" [Ref. 64]. In the Netflix documentary, "Have a Good Trip: Adventures in Psychedelics," which I highly recommend, Zach Leary, Timothy Leary's son, quotes his father saying "I learned more in four hours on mushrooms than I did in my previous 20 years in psychology [Ref. 63]."

LSD

LSD, "acid" or Lysergic Acid Diethylamide is a chemical not derived from a plant but has similar entheogenic, psychoactive properties. Albert Hofmann, a chemist working for Sandoz Pharmaceuticals in Basel, Switzerland, synthesized LSD for the first time in 1938 for use as an analeptic, or a central nervous system stimulant [Ref. 77]. It was not until 1943 when Hofmann accidentally consumed LSD that its hallucinogenic effects became known.

Hoffman rode his bike home—and experienced a range of emotions from "terror to a sense of good fortune and enjoyment." He said that behind his eyes was a "kaleidoscope of fantastic images surged in on me, alternating, variegated, opening and then closing themselves in circles and spirals, exploding in colored fountains, rearranging and hybridizing themselves in constant flux" [Ref. 77]. A house doctor examined him later and detected no serious effects from drug just dilated pupils. This first "trip" became known as "Bicycle Day" for psychedelic communities to celebrate the founding of LSD.

In the 1950s, Sandoz Pharmaceuticals gave away LSD (then called Delysid) to psychiatrists to use for medical research. In return, they shared their experiences to build data on the effects of the medicine. British doctors Ronald Sandison and Humphry Osmond, were among the first to find that it "induced mystical experiences that seemed to help shake people out of addictions and other patterns of negative thinking" [Ref. 78].

My first and only experience of "dropping" acid was with a close friend– when we spent the day in a redwood forest in Northern California. I remember this incredible rush of energy rolling through me as we playfully hiked through trees. At one point, I remember hearing music emanating from the trees, plants and Earth.

That night, we ended up at a friend's place, where the wall of her living room opened up to a redwood forest. It was so magical. She was an artist that had made several paintings while on acid decorating her walls. When I looked at them in my altered state, the image undulated in a holographic way. By the end of the night after dinner, I sat across the room from our friend who was pregnant at the time. When I looked at her, I tuned in and I could hear her baby moving in the placenta. I asked her, "did your baby just kick?" She said, "yes." Again, my ESP, "extra sensory perception" was activated from the power of this entheogen. It was a magical moment I will never forget.

An indigenous practice that is making a comeback is microdosing or that is taking about 5-10% of a full dose of a psychoactive medicine, usually psilocybin or LSD, to get the benefits of the substance without the "tripping" or psychedelic effect. Author Dr. Jim Fadiman notes in a study, just a tenth to twentieth of a normal dose lifted depression in eighty percent of people who tried antidepressant drugs before and it had failed them [Ref. 125].

Author Ayelet Waldman's book called "A Really Good Day: How Microdosing Made a Mega Difference in My Mood, My Marriage, and My Life" is about her journey of exhausting the pharmaceutical route's failure to treat her extreme mood outbursts from anxiety and bipolar disorder, causing many problems in her family life and marriage. So she goes on a 30 day trial of microdosing LSD, which is not psychedelic at this dose, but the effect is more therapeutic. The result was her mood becoming much more calm and balanced, with "some sleep disruption but nowhere close to the negative side effects of prescription drugs" (Ref. 189).

Her younger daughter says to her after her treatment with LSD, "Who are you?", "You've been much happier," "You've been controlling your emotions. Like, when you're angry, you're super-chill" (Ref. 189). Waldman is yet another success story of the power of entheogens to help heal mental and emotional trauma, creating more wellness in our lives.

Ayahuasca

Ayahuasca is served as a tea by boiling the Banisteriopsis caapi vine with the leaves of the Psychotria viridis shrub, and has been used for centuries by First Nations people from contemporary Peru, Brazil, Colombia and Ecuador for religious ritual and therapeutic purposes [Ref. 74]. Unlike other entheogens such as mushrooms and LSD, ayahuasca is not typically known for being done recreationally nor do I think it should ever be. It's very intense and its message is especially sacred, customized specifically to each user. My first experience of ingesting ayahuasca was in a sacred ceremony led by members of the

Shipibo, an ancient tribe from the Amazonian rainforest in Peru, who are credited for sharing their sacred medicine with foreigners [Ref. 75].

There are many things I could say about my mystical journey with ayahuasca. If you desire to try it, please find a sacred ceremony or center, creating a safe container for your healing journey. In preparation for the ceremony, I did the normal abstaining from sex, drugs, alcohol and meat days a few weeks beforehand. Then before actually ingesting the tea, we spend hours praying, singing *icaros* or sacred chants and consume sacred tobacco in various forms.

One form is called rapé (rah-pay), a powdered form of tobacco that is blown into or snorted up the nose in each nostril. The effect is to detox the body and mind as well to calm and ground you before partaking in ayahuasca. In our ceremony, we used liquid tobacco. I can still remember the way it burned my nose, head and how my throat tingled. But then moments later, it felt like each side of my brain opened like a flower blooming. It was an amazing feeling. The power of these plant medicines is undeniable and when you experience it for yourself, you will understand how truly related we are to the Earth.

After the preparation, in a circle of about 20 participants, we sat in silence as each person went to the center of the circle to ingest the tea. There were wastebaskets beside each cushion in the event of purging or vomiting which is a part of the purification. Once I ingested the tea and sat down, it took some time to feel anything. But when I did many intense visions of my past, present and future unfolded in my mind's eye, each with their own message about my purpose, my power and where I need to heal and grow. Powerful waves of energy were streaming through me and at one point I felt a serpent-like energy scanning my body for imbalances to purge. I have never felt the intelligence of a plant like that before.

Ana Maria, one of the leaders of the ceremony shared that this medicine helped her to purge illnesses that she didn't even know she had. About 30 minutes into the journey, several people on the other side of the room began to vomit. I was on the quiet side of the room where everyone was clearly having an intense internal experience. Some people were making noises. It was an intense high that would last until sunrise. As the sun rose, I drank more water as some experienced friends said to wait at the end if possible since water will make you purge. When I finally did, I purged out a blood clot and felt better afterwards.

By morning, we ended the ceremony in prayer, then we were free to eat something light or take a walk in nature to process the evening. When I found myself surrounded by the trees and sunlight, I could feel sweet spirits around me whispering loving words like "I love you," "you are beautiful," "you are amazing" and so on. Wow! Maybe that's what the plants are already saying to us but by ingesting the plants we can tune into a frequency we may not normally have access to. Entheogens can enhance psychic abilities like telepathy as well.

In Shipibo culture, the shamans or curanderos are healers who use plant-based medicines to treat illnesses that have physical, mental, and spiritual causes [Ref. 75]. They believe that ayahuasca possesses "divinatory properties" that allow them to "communicate with spirits of nature and see another person's metaphysical blockages." Shamans communicate with the spiritual world to "alleviate traumas affecting the soul or spirit [that] are believed to restore the physical body of the individual to balance and wholeness" [Ref. 76]. In these ceremonies, the curanderos also ingest ayahuasca to attune deeper into the spirit realm and see where the imbalances lie in the participant to help bring them back into balance. Healing the psychic spiritual root cause of an illness is what shamanism and the use of plant medicines are all about.

Psychoactive Cacti: Mescaline, Peyote, Wachuma and San Pedro

The elegant and strange prickly plant known as the cactus has also been used for its entheogenic properties for over 5,000 years in religious and spiritual ceremonies by indigenous people in Mesoamerica, particularly in Mexico, Peru and Ecuador [Ref. 84]. The active compound, mescaline, is found in peyote and San Pedro. It has similar effects to psilocybin and LSD, in that it creates mind-altering states with visuals, heightens the senses and transforms one's sense of time and self-awareness. And like all entheogens it affects serotonin levels, creating feelings of happiness, wellness and connection.

According to experiences from peyote users, it is said to promote profound spiritual insights, increase creative problem-solving abilities, relieve anxiety, reduce suicidal thoughts and reduce addiction to harmful substances [Ref. 124]. Peyote, like all entheogens, creates a deeper connection of the individual to the world around them and has reportedly made people less violent and more eco-conscious by adopting behaviors like veganism and recycling [Ref. 124].

There is archaeological evidence of fossilized peyote in caves used in ceremonies, as well as large artworks that honored peyote dating to over 3,000-5,000 years ago [Ref. 85]. The Huichol Tribe, indigenous to Mexico, believed that "all plants were a gift from God and that peyote had a special divine gift with magical powers" [Ref. 85]. Huichol would make pilgrimages every year to Wirikuta, Mexico where peyote grows in mass quantities [Ref. 85].

It was not until 1519, when Spanish conquistador Herman Corte, who "conquered" the Aztecs, that Peyote became a problem. The Spaniards saw peyote as "witchcraft" and a threat since those who used it seemed to not show "fear or hunger." They feared it would aid the Aztecs to revolt [Ref. 85]. By 1620, peyote became illegal and "punishable by death" [Ref. 85]. Indigenous American natives continued to pass along the knowledge of peyote to future generations in secrecy to maintain their legacy.

Word got to Europe about peyote in the late 1800s, when German doctor--Arthur Heffter got his hands on peyote and started his own research on its psychoactive effects [Ref. 85]. Heffter was first to isolate the active compound in peyote. He named it mescaline in honor of the Mescalero Apache tribe whose land provided the "peyote buttons" for his research [Ref. 85]. Then in 1919 German chemist Ernst Spath discovered how to synthesize mescaline [Ref. 84]. In the early 1950s, Canadian, Dr. Humphrey Osmond, began to experiment with mescaline to treat psychiatric conditions which encouraged more medical professionals to follow suit.

In 1953, author Aldous Huxley was interested in using it creatively. Under the supervision of Dr. Humphrey, Huxley took 400 mg of mescaline and later documented his detailed experience in his book, "Doors of Perception," one of my favorite short books [Ref. 84]. His book helped spread its popularity to the Western world during the 1960s, yet it was still harder to find than LSD because it is hard to make [Ref. 85]. In 1960, Alexander Shulgin tried mescaline and loved it so much that he "devoted his career to discovering phenylethylamines and other alkaloids," which led to his creation of MDMA [Ref. 85].

Wachuma is a derivative of San Pedro, known as the "heart of the Jaguar" connecting us deeper to our emotions, from the heights of Peruvian Andes mountains, dating back to over 4000 years. I was able to sit with this medicine recently and had a very profound experience, helping me to return to my essence and merge with God consciousness.

I prepared for the ceremony for four weeks using rapeh, kambo and deep, one on one meditative sessions with my curandera or plant medicine healer and fasting a week prior to my ceremony.

Rapeh is a shamanic sacred medicine from the Amazon that comes as a powdered form of tobacco mixed with other medicines like tree barks. It is inhaled through the nose and has a grounding effect that helps balance and purify our consciousness, connecting us with source and our higher self.

Kambo is a powerful detoxification protocol used by ancient Amazonian Tribes. It is used to eliminate toxins in the lymphatic system and to increase the body's natural ability to heal itself, increasing vitality in body and mind. It is known to help heal a host of maladies that affect the mind, emotions and body.

As with tradition, I prepared my body, mind and spirit before sitting with Wachuma by working with my curandera, using rapeh, kambo, meditation, fasting and temazcal, which is a sweat lodge, to detox the body by profusely sweating while setting intentions through prayer.

As opposed to ayahuasca, which is considered the "grandmother" medicine, Wachuma is considered the "grandfather" medicine and in my experience, much more gentle. The trip can last over 10 hours and is taken as a tea which can also make you purge. Not a visually-driven experience like Ayahuasca or mushrooms, Wachuma gave me this embodied, inner knowing and confidence in my own wisdom and self mastery. It helped me to access a deeper wisdom within myself, giving me more clarity on how to navigate certain emotional issues I needed to heal.

Bufo

Bufo is a toxin derived from the venom secreted from the *Bufo alvarius* toad from the Sonoran Desert in Mexico, California and Arizona that is smoked. Using psychoactive substances from various toads like the *Bufo marinus* date back as far as 2000 BCE represented in the art of the Olmecs, Mayans and Aztecs (Ref. 190).

The Yaqui people of this region call this medicine "Koarepa" and consider the *Bufo alvarius* toad, sacred, weaving it into their art, stories and rituals. Bufo contains 5-MeO-DMT, which is about five times stronger than DMT, called the "spirit molecule." It's a more short-lived experience of 20-30 minutes, as opposed to DMT which can last hours, but the effect is immense.

DMT is found in many parts of the body like the lungs, heart, spinal cord and more (Ref. 191) "DMT: The Spirit Molecule," written by clinical psychiatrist Rick Strassman in 2000, theorized that the pineal gland or "third eye" releases DMT when we are born and for a few hours when die (Ref. 191).

Recently, I had my first experience sitting with Bufo. I experienced the purest form of love or God consciousness and wondered if this is where we go when we die.

With my eyes closed, I was in a realm with no form and no boundaries, just a unified field of vibratory rainbow-colored frequencies with a brilliant glowing light behind it. I was speechless. All I could do was moan from the unspeakable beauty and love I felt. It was a powerfully transformative experience that gave me a profound connection to all life.

I will never be the same.

MDMA

I can recall the times I took ecstasy also known as MDMA or molly, in my 20s and 30s. Also referred to as "rolling" when you are on the drug typically used socially at a party. The effect varied in intensity depending on the purity of the drug but the effect was typically the same, an overwhelming feeling of intense love. If you are normally shy, you won't be anymore. And it's not like a rush of courage you get from alcohol, it's a more energized feeling with a blissful sense that the world and the people in it are beautiful. Your entire body can become a source of arousal and easily stimulated, so it is wise to practice set and setting to ensure no undesired effects or outcomes happen.

Ecstasy refers to the tablet form, where MDMA (the active substance) is diluted with another drug such as "amphetamine, cocaine, caffeine, bath salts or even ketamine" in some cases [Ref. 82]. Depending on the purity and what it's mixed with, the effects of ecstasy can have more of an unpredictable effect. Powdered MDMA, usually in a capsule, is the purest form of the drug also known as 3-4 methylenedioxymethamphetamine. It's a synthetic, psychoactive drug that has an energetic and hallucinogenic effect that was first created in 1912 as an appetite suppressant in Germany [Ref. 80]. MDMA enhances levels of oxytocin which is known as "the love hormone" because it "increases trust, promotes social bonding, and fosters compassion" [Ref. 81].

I recall the difference I felt when doing ecstasy versus MDMA. When I was younger, I did the tablet form ecstasy and it was always a mystery how it would affect you. It could make you excited or relaxed depending on what it was mixed with then how much pure MDMA was in it. When I became older and more discerning about what I put in my body, I would only take MDMA also known as molly which is pure MDMA. In these experiences, there was no rocky start of anxiety like in the case of ecstasy, but a clean and clear beginning and end that only left me with enhanced feelings of empathy, sensuality and connection to oneself and others. The recovery was also night and day, with ecstasy having a very harsh recovery period versus MDMA.

Chemist and psychopharmacologist Alexander "Sasha" Shulgin who created MDMA in the 1960s, after his inspired experience on mescaline, claimed that MDMA was his "tamed" version of mescaline, less intense and not lasting as long [Ref. 85]. By the 1970s up until today, MDMA has become a dance club drug, enhancing the music dance experience for generations. PiHKAL: A Chemical Love Story is a book where the late Alexander Shulgin and his wife Ann Shulgin, also a psychopharmacologist, documented their decades of MDMA use and other psychedelics to enhance intimacy in their relationship. "PiHKAL" is an acronym for "Phenethylamines I Have Known And Loved" [Ref. 86].

MDMA has been used in recent years to treat mental health issues like PTSD. In one case, a young female who suffered from PTSD and was unresponsive to conventional forms of therapy, was administered pure MDMA with the support of two psychotherapists [Ref. 83]. With the aid of MDMA, she was able to revisit painful, traumatic moments without fear and anxiety and was able to see it through a new lens where she developed compassion for herself [Ref. 83].

How Psychedelics Can Help Save the World

Entheogenic use causes "ego dissolution" or "ego death" or the dissolving of the boundaries between ourselves, other people, nature and with the entire Universe or God promoting a unified awareness. Author and ethnopharmacologist Dennis McKenna says "Psychedelics are not suppressed because they are dangerous to users; they're suppressed because they provoke unconventional thought, which threatens any number of elites and institutions that would rather do our thinking for us."

In the 1960s, the hippie peace movement of "Make Love, Not War," was born on the use of psychedelics like cannabis and LSD, that helped to expand the consciousness of the youth to lead the way in promoting global peace in the face of the Vietnam War. This "consciousness revolution" would also lead to the feminist movement, ecology movement, gay liberation movement and the awakening is still happening [Ref. 63].

A book recently published entitled, "How Psychedelics Can Help Save the World: Visionary and Indigenous Voices Speak Out" with over 25 contributors, from psychic visionaries to indigenous people like Dennis McKenna and Grandmother Maria Alice, believe that these powerful earth-based medicines can heal the fear and separation, at the root of oppression, violence and conflict, and help birth a new consciousness that promotes a reconnection to spirit, Nature and bring about global peace and harmony.

Chapter 4: Reflections:
How can entheogens help you heal your emotional trauma?

Chapter 5

Gender and Sexuality: Loving the Spectrum of Who We Are and Who We Desire

What is Gender and Sexuality?

Gender and sexuality have risen in importance in the last 50 years due to more people wanting to choose how to socially and culturally identify themselves and how they want to be identified by society.

Gender is about how one identifies socially and culturally as opposed to biological traits and body parts. Sexuality is about how one expresses one's gender and who one chooses to mate with.

The term "heterosexuality" did not even come into Western thought until the early 1900s when Dorland's Medical Dictionary defined heterosexuality as an "abnormal or perverted appetite toward the opposite sex" [Ref. 87]. In the 1920s, it appeared in Merriam Webster's dictionary with a meaning similar to the medical definition. Only in 1934 was the definition of heterosexuality changed to the "manifestation of sexual passion for one of the opposite sex; normal sexuality" [Ref. 87].

From this social construction, the idea of "heteronormativity" is that heterosexuality is "normal" and the standard. So if someone deviates from this, they are abnormal or deemed an outcast. This idea has caused many non-conforming, fluid identifying humans a lot of suffering. They endure exclusion, discrimination and violence, from their families, societies, institutions and religions. The concepts of gender fluidity and diverse sexualities are not new. Various ancient societies had their own terms like "two-spirit" from indigenous Mesoamerican people and "third gender" from indigenous people from the Pacific islands to identify those who had a more fluid gender beyond the male/female binary.

Binary means only two options. Today, when one identifies as non-binary, it means they do not fit in either box. According to writer Ariel David, the "pluralistic notion of diverse non-conforming gender identities in older traditional cultures was crushed by Western Colonial rule in which European concepts, based on Judeo-Christian values were 'forcibly introduced'" [Ref. 97].

Queer theorist Dave Halperin explains "sex has no history" as it is "rooted in the functions of the body" [Ref. 87]. Whereas sexuality expresses a form of "cultural production" that has to do with the "naming and categorizing of those (sexual) acts, and those who practice those acts" [Ref. 87]. We can look at history and see ancient patterns across the globe that included a diversity of sexual and gender identities. It is clear that religion has played a large part in spreading the ignorance and hate of homophobia and transphobia. Being Catholic as a queer person was traumatizing for me after being taught that I was evil and going to hell because of my sexuality.

These types of inhumane, homophobic beliefs are a source of mental illness, violence, discrimination and suicide within queer communities. That's why it is so important to discover the truth for ourselves to feel supported and empowered in being who we are.

Practicing Nichiren Buddhism for over 15 years has helped to heal some of this trauma. This profound religion from Japan recognizes each human with equal potential and value regardless of gender, sexuality, race, class, age or any other varying trait. It is the most humanistic modern religion I know. Because of its healing philosophies, practices and accepting communities, I have been able to heal a lot of the internalized hate and judgment I grew up with and still deal with from society.

People are complex and our labels should accurately reflect who we are, not what social structures want us to be. Today, gender identities can now include but are not limited to "male, female, transgender, gender neutral, non-binary, agender, pangender, genderqueer, two-spirit, third gender, and all, none or a combination of these" [Ref. 91]. Among the young people of "Gen Z," when I speak to some from the San Francisco Bay Area, after asking what your name is, the next question asked is, "what is your pronoun?" Our society is changing to be more inclusive and sensitive to those who fit outside of the gender binary. This is also clear with more gender neutral bathrooms emerging all over the world where more queer people live. Any step in the direction of acknowledging the human rights of our diversity is a step towards world peace.

Sexualities can include but are not limited to heterosexual, gay, lesbian, bisexual and queer, which is everything but heterosexual. Emerging sexuality identities are pansexual; one who is attracted to any gender and sexuality, questioning; one who is exploring their sexual orientation, heteroflexible; a heterosexual that may experience an attraction outside of that, demisexual; one who must feel a strong emotional connection to feel sexual, sapiosexual; one who must feel a strong mental connection to feel sexual, asexual; one who feels a lack of romantic attraction to others and many more out there, you can explore and discover [Ref. 93].

The word "queer" was once used as a derogatory term toward gay people. It was reclaimed by the LGBTQ+ (Lesbian, Gay, Bisexual, Trans, Queer) community after the Stonewall Riots in 1969, where people began to chant, "We're here. We're queer. Get used to it!" [Ref. 89] Reclaiming the word "queer," meaning strange or weird, was born out of the need to redefine what is "normal" and come out of the margins into the center of visibility.

Abundant Evidence of Gender and Sexuality Diversity

When I started researching historic evidence on this topic, it was overwhelming to see how much we are not taught. I can only cite a few examples here but as with all the themes I explore in this book, please do your own research if you are interested in learning more. There is documented evidence that within indigenous Native

American Pan-Tribal culture, there were "more than 100 different gender expressions" [Ref. 97].

In traditional Jewish rabbinical writings, "six different genders were recognized: the main gender binary, plus four other genders that can only really be understood as Intersex/intersexual" [Ref. 97]. In ancient cultures in "Mesopotamia, Sumerian, Assyria, Babylonia and Akkadian there is historical evidence (including texts from 4500 BC) that document priests-priestesses known as 'Gala', a Male-to-Female priesthood that was accepted as sacred and given reverence" [Ref. 97].

In native Hawai'i and other Polynesian societies, māhū were men who formed relationships with men and were more inclined to take on the gender roles of women like cooking, cleaning, caretaking, etc [Ref. 88]. Moe aikāne relationships is a pre-colonial term used to describe intimate relationships between those of the same gender, used especially among royalty and chiefs.

In 1564, French explorer, René Goulaine de Laudonnière and his team, came to a place that is now known as Florida, which was homeland to the Timucua. de Laudonnière stated after being exhausted from travel, "We met an Indian woman of tall stature, who also was a Hermaphrodite, who came before us with a great vessel, full of clear fountain water, which she greatly refreshed us" [Ref. 88].

"Hermaphrodite" is an outdated term for someone who is "intersex" or that possesses both female and male biological traits. In this historical account, it is unknown if they were intersex or perhaps they were just gender fluid so the terminology used may be inaccurate. Either way, more evidence that this human condition is neither novel or abnormal but indeed a part of our natural history that has been omitted.

Seahorses also disrupt our human gender roles when it comes to pregnancy. The gender roles are switched where the female produces eggs then transfers them into the male's "brood pouch," which the male fertilizes, then holds the embryos until it's their time to be birthed. In this species, the male gives birth to the offspring which happens in other aquatic species as well (Ref. 192).

Within Native American and First Nations communities, "two spirit" or "two-spirited" is used in reference to both male-bodied and female-bodied native people who are a mixture of the standard roles of men and women [Ref. 88]. "Two-spirit males have been documented in at least 155 tribes; in about a third of these there is a recognized status for females who adopted a masculine lifestyle as well" [Ref. 88].

As you can see, these similar identification matters found in modern day society have been in practice in ancient and modern day cultures of the people indigenous to the Americas. As seen in the Western world where only a two-gender binary exists of male/female is "natural" based on sexual organs, "many native societies are capable of accommodating three, four, and possibly more genders, or having a gender system characterized by fluidity, transformation, and individual variation" [Ref. 88].

When talking about the origins of gender, gender roles and sexuality among humans, we must also look at how this all plays out in the animal world. On a visit to the Philippines, I recall seeing a male billy goat happily penetrating another billy goat from behind. Yes, queer relations have existed in the animal world since the beginning of time as well.

Same-sex behavior dates back to 322 B.C. when Aristotle wrote about various species of birds copulating with the same sex [Ref.

96]. In Egypt, same-sex relations among partridges and intersex hyenas can be found in the Hieroglyphics of Horapollo in the 4th century A.D. Also, "clownfish, wrasses, moray eels, gobies and other fish species are known to change sex during their lives, including reproductive functions" [Ref. 96].

According to Bruce Bagemihl, a Canadian biologist and author of the book "Biological Exuberance: Animal Homosexuality and Natural Diversity" says "same-sex behavior [in the animal kingdom] (comprising of courtship, sexual, pair-bonding, and parental activities) is enormous and has been documented in over 450 species of animals worldwide" [Ref. 96]. Some of these animals include primates, penguins, giraffes, elephants, dolphins, lions, birds, bats, bison, insects and many other species that engage in same-sex relationships.

In 2003, his book on homosexuality in animals was cited by the American Psychiatric Association (APA) in their brief to the United States Supreme Court in *Lawrence v. Texas*, the case which ultimately struck down sodomy laws across the United States. Sodomy laws targeted same-sex acts and certain sex acts as illegal since the 17th century claiming they were "unnatural" and "immoral."

The decriminalization of same-sex acts in the US has only come in the last century. Same-sex behavior was deemed as a mental disorder by the American Psychiatric Association from 1968-1973 in the DSM or Diagnostic and Statistical Manual of Mental Disorders. It was not removed completely from the DSM until 1987 [Ref. 126].

As you can see, diversity of gender and sexuality identities is not a human invention but a fact of nature since humans began to document their experiences. If more people understood these hidden parts of our history, perhaps we could have more peace, harmony and a safer place for people who do not conform to prescribed identities of who we are "supposed" to be and enjoy the freedom to be who we really are.

Human Rights for LGBTQ+ People and Women

It is no secret that queer people, from antiquity to today, have been demonized, violated and ostracized by religions, governments, laws, institutions and ignorant people. Even today, it is illegal in some countries to be gay and even punishable by death.

The truth of who we are is defined by us, not by those who seek to devalue our humanity and cause us harm. I believe in empowerment, inclusion and in the retelling of our stories that confirm our human dignity and innate worthiness.

The Stonewall Riots started on June 29, 1969 was a pivotal moment in the progress for gay human rights. In the 1960s and prior to that, New York was not a safe place for queer people as the "solicitation of same-sex relations was illegal in New York City" [Ref. 90]. The Stonewall Inn, where the riots began, was in Greenwich Village, New York City, and frequented by queer people. It was raided and its staff and patrons were dragged out of the bar by police, which caused the community to riot against the police, tired of their mistreatment and social discrimination. The protests would last for six days, involving thousands of people [Ref. 90].

Christopher Street Liberation Day began on the one year anniversary of Stonewall Riots on June 28, 1970. It was America's first gay pride parade, where thousands of people marched in the streets of Manhattan from the Stonewall Inn to Central Park, chanting 'Say it loud, gay is proud'" [Ref. 90]. Marsha P. Johnson was a prominent trans activist and artist in this movement being called the "Mayor of Christopher Street," whose work gained more visibility for the trans community.

The riots sparked many gay human rights organizations to emerge and fight for queer acceptance and visibility including GLAAD, (Gay & Lesbian Alliance Against Defamation), Human Rights Campaign (HRC) and Gay Liberation Front [Ref. 90]. Many queer human rights organizations, gay pride parades and the fight for equal rights for gay people all over the world have been inspired by this one event.

In 2016, Barack Obama made Christopher Street a national landmark for gay human rights [Ref. 90]. A year before this on June 26, 2015, gay marriage was legalized by the US Supreme Court under President Obama. He stated "Love is love. This ruling is a victory for America. It affirms what millions of Americans already believe in their hearts: when all Americans are treated as equal, we are all more free" [Ref. 92].

It may be hard for some people to understand what a big deal legal marriage is for many queer people. I was raised in a religious family, where my sexuality and who I love was simply denied. Being excluded as the norm, was very painful to bear.

I was 37 when gay marriage passed and it was not until that moment, I realized that I could marry another woman and have a family if I wanted. This freedom and right that heterosexual people enjoy was now a reality for fellow human beings, someone queer like me. Progress.

Since I was a child, I have found it offensive and inaccurate that most world religions depict God as only a man. Is not childbirth one of the most divine, Godly human activities? And isn't it a fact that all humans passed through the vagina of a woman to live? Then why not also depict God as female as well.

In Nichiren Buddhism, the religion I practice, our vision of divinity is the gohonzon, which is an ancient scroll that depicts the totality of life, death, good and bad. It is the recognition of the beauty and complexity of existence that transcends the binary of male/female. I have found this depiction of divinity to be more accurate and less damaging to make one gender feel superior over another then create ideologies and behaviors that justify such discrimination. This is why some people don't like "major" religions and I get it.

Around the world, sexist, homophobic and transphobic religions, political systems and social institutions treat women as inferior to justify male domination. In 2023 in Iran, women, by the tens of thousands, were jailed and some were killed for not wearing a hijab (head covering) in public.

These institutions also exclude those who exist beyond the gender binary or trans people, normalizing exclusion and hatred. This is the cause of much suffering, discrimination, violence and death within our communities.

In 2016, the U.S. military lifted its ban on transgender people serving openly, a month after Eric Fanning became secretary of the Army and the first openly gay secretary of a U.S. military branch [Ref. 94]. In the last few years, the ACLU or American Civil Liberties Union, states there are 409 anti-LGBTQ bills in US state legislatures from allowing discrimination to occur in places of business and employment to banning drag shows and censoring freedom of speech [Ref. 127].

A few of my trans Asian friends, who are female-to-male (FTM), both agree that it was easier for them to come out as a gay female than when they came out as a female to male. They admitted to feeling dysphoric in their born bodies that did not match their consciousness.

My friend admitted to me that it was hard feeling on the border of male and female, being constantly misgendered. So the desire to transition was to feel comfortable in their own body and experience as well as fit into the binary that made the most sense to them which was as a male.

There are many variations of trans identity– like choosing which pronouns feel appropriate, gender presentation and expression and hormonal injection and/or gender reassignment, which in some cases is covered by health insurance.

The most important thing we can do as allies to trans people, is to listen to their experiences, fully accept and respect their identity and their choices in how they wish to be named and express their gender. The same respect that all people should be given.

I want to impart this message especially to cisgendered men and cisgendered women (cis meaning those assigned at birth) and heterosexual people. It is enough for LGBTQ+ people to deal with hatred and discrimination from society or from their families. Please consider each human life as sacred and worthy of respect. As humans, we are all worthy of equal, humane treatment regardless of our differences. What if they were your child? Would you judge them or accept them for who they are and what makes them happy?

No one is God and therefore no one should not feel empowered or justified to pass judgment on or tell queer people who we are or how we should feel or live. It is everyone's human right to live their lives that feels natural to them. Learning to love and accept those who are different from us, is the only way we can create peace in our world. Compassion is the compass we must use to navigate the differences of our human experience.

Androgyny Is Both Masculine and Feminine

When we talk about gender and sexuality, there is masculine and feminine energy which all genders possess but in various proportions for each person. I believe gender and sexuality is on a continuum that can vary depending on what stage someone is in their life. Masculine energy, typically associated with men but not limited to, is action-oriented, rational, mentally and physically strong, protective and productive. Feminine energy, typically associated with women but not limited to, is nurturing, emotionally intelligent, intuitive, sensitive, compassionate and cooperative.

In my opinion, the notion of God/Goddess or divinity, is the dynamic balance of masculine and feminine energy, sometimes called "androgyny." All my life, I have always been drawn to masculine women and feminine men. To be born with one nature then to nurture the part of us that may not be as natural and to find balance in oneself is to me to be the closest to God or divine-like. I have always felt more comfort in men who are nurturing and compassionate and with women who are strong, smart and independent.

Gender identities where men are only encouraged to embody the stereotypical masculine traits of physical strength and aggression are unbalanced and can be damaging, by affirming toxic behavior that can lead to violence. The same goes for women, who only cultivate traditionally feminine qualities where they are a "damsel in distress," emotionally volatile, easily moved to fears and tears, in need of a man to feel grounded and protected. This stereotype seen in older literature and films and its remnants feed into the traditional gender roles that can be imbalanced and unhealthy. I think having a balance of masculine and feminine energies within each person can only contribute to healthier relationships and a healthier society. In the version of my story, the "female in distress" is strong enough to save herself.

So what is androgyny? Androgyny is the identity given to those who transcend the gender binary of male and female, AND contain both masculine and feminine qualities, or "gender-benders." People are fascinated by androgyny. To live beyond the conformity and limits of the gender binary is liberation. Throughout history especially in music and the arts, androgynous artists have broken new ground and become legends.

LGBTQ-Centered Art Opens More Doors for Equality

A short list of legendary gender-bending artists include Frida Kahlo, Prince, Michael Jackson, Boy George, Freddie Mercury, Annie Lennox, RuPaul, Andy Warhol and David Bowie, to name a few.

What's fascinating is that not all of these artists were "gay." Diversity in gender expression and sexuality can be separate and/or joined. But the ones who were queer are like superheroes to queer people, for the way they broke new ground in the face of discrimination to become legends whose work is still relevant today. Queer artistic representation is a huge part in gaining human rights for queer people globally to be seen and respected and feel safe for who we truly are.

Many artists opened the door, exposing the public to more diverse gender expressions and sexualities. In 1975, Tim Curry starred in the musical film, "The Rocky Horror Picture Show" and dressed in drag or that is a man who wears women's makeup and clothing.

When I was just an adolescent, my cool older cousin took me to a weekly screening where people came religiously dressed in costumes and re-enacted every scene from the movie also known as a "shadowcast." It was a ground-breaking film for the queer community that gave us a sense of empowerment and belonging by seeing ourselves on the big screen.

Some notable mentions of films that broke ground and featured androgynous characters is the award-winning film, including 6 Academy award nominations and one win for best costume design, was "Some Like It Hot" from 1959, starring Marilyn Monroe, Tony Curtis and Jack Lemmon. The two male leads are musicians running from the mafia after witnessing a crime, so they dress as women in an all-female band to escape.

Another award-winning film, with 5 Academy award nominations and one win for best music, was "Yentl" which came out in 1983, starring Barbara Streisand, where she dresses as a man to be able to receive the same education rights in a restrictive religious school in the Jewish community.

A year earlier in 1982, another award-winning film with 10 Academy award nominations and one win for best supporting actress to Jessica Lange was "Tootsie," starring Dustin Hoffman, as a down-on-his-luck actor who dresses up as a woman to get a role in a daytime drama. Once s/he gets the role, s/he begins to inspire other women to break free from the control of men.

In 1990, the historic award-winning documentary, "Paris Is Burning," documents the warm community and vital support within the trans community representing "ball(room) culture" in New York City from the mid-to-late 1980's among the LGBTQ+ African-American and Latino communities, starring renowned pioneers like Willie Ninja, Dorian Corey and Pepper LaBeija.

In "ball culture," each group from "houses" compete in elaborate balls expressing themselves through dance like voguing, walking and fashion. A new TV show that came out in 2020 on HBO Max called, "Legendary" continues to represent competitions and artistry of ball culture at its finest, with a $100,000 cash prize to the winning house.

More TV shows that pioneered queer representation and inspired queer people to feel seen and heard by witnessing our stories in the mainstream are The L Word, Noah's Arc, Queer As Folk, Ellen, RuPaul's Drag Race and so on.

In the last thirty years, many TV shows have had more realistic queer characters represented to help to facilitate more equal rights for LGBTQ people. But seen in the numerous bills that mostly Republicans are trying to pass discriminatory laws against the LGBTQ+ community, there is still more work to do in garnering equal human rights for queer people in the US and worldwide. Until it is safe to be gay in all places of this big beautiful world, we will continue to represent our stories and create safe spaces for our voices to be heard.

Some of my favorite queer writers that were visible when our stories were kept in the dark out of fear and protection are Nikki Giovanni, bell hooks, James Baldwin, Audre Lorde, Adrienne Rich, Walt Whitman, Virginia Woolf, beatnik poets Allen Ginsberg and Jack Kerouac, Langston Hughes, June Jordan, Frederico Garcia Lorca and Yukio Mishima.

In 1956, "Giovanni's Room" was released by prolific writer, James Baldwin, about a bisexual American expat living in Paris who is still coming to terms with his sexuality. Groundbreaking for its time, the book represents the internal conflict the main character David faces between being gay and what he is told he is "supposed" to be by society and by his family. This timeless theme really resonated with me in my 20s when I gay and closeted for fear of rejection, being raised in a Filipino Catholic family and generally homophobic community. The book helped to normalize my experience and realize that I was not alone.

From her poem entitled "II" from Twenty-One Love Poems, award-winning lesbian poet, Adrienne Rich, writes "You've kissed my hair to wake me. I dreamed you were a poem, I say, a poem I wanted to show someone..and I laugh and fall, dreaming again of the desire to show you to everyone I love, to move openly together in the pull of gravity, which is not simple" [Ref. 98]. I completely relate to her fear of being out as a lesbian with her female lover. I had my first girlfriend when I was 18 and she was 24. We were together for 3 years and were both closeted to our families, so hiding who we were was a way of life. Luckily, we moved away to Chicago when we began dating so being out to our friends in a new city was a safe place for us.

I did not come out to my family until I was 26 out of fear of being disowned because my parents were devout Catholics. To my surprise when I finally came out, my parents already knew I was gay–and accepted me unconditionally. I was fortunate but for many, "coming out of the closet," by telling your family and community you are gay, can be a painful, isolating and a risky situation. Some who come out, face judgment, discrimination or in extreme cases, violence. That is why queer artists and public figures who make us more visible by telling our stories, are key in making the world a safer place for us to exist.

The groundbreaking poetry anthology, "This Bridge Called My Back" from 1981, captures the voices and experiences of female poets of color from African-American, Native American, Asian American and Latina American descent, speaking from the intersectionality of feminism, race, sexuality and class. I encountered this book in my 20s, when I was performing as a spoken word artist in the San Francisco Bay Area. In 2001, at the 20th Anniversary event of "This Bridge Called My Back," in San Francisco, I was featured as a performance poet. There I met other queers, queer allies and women of color poets; this launched me into performing my poetry and sharing my unique story. The opportunity to represent as a queer poet of color was pivotal in empowering and shaping my voice as an artist for years to come.

Legendary musicians, both queer and queer allies, who pioneered queer representation with their music and message normalizing queer experiences were pioneers like Ma Rainey, Bessie Smith, Little Richard, Liberace, Freddie Mercury of Queen, Elton John and Barry Manilow to modern musicians like Michael Stipe of R.E.M., Lil Nas X, Lady Gaga, Brandi Carlile, K.D. Lang, Melissa Etheridge, Sam Smith, Ricky Martin, Meshell N'degeocello, Tracey Chapman, Queen Latifah, Janelle Monae, Frank Ocean, Tyler, the Creator, Kaytranada, Big Freedia, Billy Porter, Miley Cyrus, Madonna, Cyndi Lauper and ABBA, with their queer anthem "Dancing Queen."

As you can see, it would be impossible to name every queer artist but I did my best to represent those who made it safer for us to be who we are publicly.

Lastly, I want to mention two of my favorite queer singers, the late Luther Vandross and George Michael. Award-winning singer, Luther Vandross, noted for his love songs to the ladies, never came out, but my "gay-dar" (an intuition about people's sexuality) always went off with him. After his death in 2005, close friends confirmed he only had a few relationships in his life, and one was a long-term relationship with a man. Patti Labelle said in 2017 that he was in fact gay [Ref. 99]. It is speculated that he didn't want to upset his lady fans, nor his Mother [Ref. 99]. I can only imagine how painful and lonely that must have been, being a superstar while living in the closet his entire life. Respect and peace to his memory, musical legacy and the sacrifices he made to feel safe.

Cultural icon, sex symbol and award-winning singer, George Michael, also widely known for his love songs to women like "Careless Whisper," was known for being heterosexual for the early part of his career. Then in 1999, he courageously came out in an interview with the Advocate, saying, "falling in love with a man ended his conflict over bisexuality..I never had a moral problem with being gay..I thought I had fallen in love with a woman a couple of times. Then I fell in love with a man, and realized that none of those things had been love" [Ref. 99]. In multiple interviews later from 2007-2009, Michael said that he hid his sexuality to not upset his mother then later confirmed his realization that he was in fact gay, not bisexual [Ref. 99].

But for me it was in 1996, before his "coming-out announcement," when he released his album, "Older" that I *knew* he was gay. First of all, that was the year I had partnered with my first girlfriend and we absolutely loved the album. Not just because it was sonically beautiful and the lyrics were deep and meaningful as only George Michael could do. If you listen carefully, every song is written to a man. I was so inspired! Here he was the global superstar I adored for so long and he comes out through his music.

From his lyrics, you can really hear the pain some of his male lovers put him through. In the title cut "Older," "Fast Love" and the touching song "Jesus to a Child" which was a song about one of his lovers, Anselmo Feleppa, who died in 1993. This album remains one of my favorites to this day for its honesty and clarity. George Michael's reflection of queer identity, expressing same-sex desire and love so unapologetically and eloquently left me feeling seen, heard and empowered.

Chapter 5: Reflections:
How can you support more inclusion of gender and sexuality diversity in your community?

Chapter 6

Love and Relationships: Self-Love, Intimacy and the Ways We Mate and Relate

Loving Ourselves as the Starting Point

When talking about love, it's key to start with the most important form of love, self-love. I think the lack of acknowledgment of how important self-love is to our health, happiness and peace in popular culture could perhaps be one of the reasons why dysfunctional relationships, poor mental health and substance abuse are so high.

Many media images and messages reinforce values of materialism and judgment that can trigger insecurities about how we look, how much money we make, what kind of car we drive and so on. Be mindful of your media diet and what you ingest as it influences your mental health and how you see yourself.

During her Mama's Gun tour, award-winning soul singer Erykah Badu, said during her concert that network TV had two messages, "Fear and buy shit." She is referring to how the news only reports negative stories usually about violence that incite fear then commercials that just program people to be consumers and go shopping. Time to turn the TV off, tune in to your own frequency and see beyond the "prescribed" life we are taught.

In her song "Love," Badu says there are only 2 emotions "fear and love, and all other emotions stem from them." Inspirational writer and speaker, Iyanla Vanzant also says, "There are only two emotions: love and fear. Love is divine. Love is the activity of God, and the only energy in which God exists. Fear, on the other hand, is a tool of the ego, which is the foundation of the belief that we are separate from God, separate from each other, and generally inferior or inadequate" [Ref. 103].

How do we choose love over fear? Where are we taught how to love ourselves and how to cultivate and maintain it? My book is an offering toward answering these questions. Because to me, love is an action, so what better way to embody self-love than to first learn to care for your mental, emotional, physical and spiritual well-being.

I believe our relationships with others are a reflection of our relationships to ourselves. The common saying "Hurt people hurt people" is so true. In my family, some of the most hurtful people were the ones who were unhappy in their own lives or ones who were judgmental or constant complainers. What if we put as much work into healing and caring for ourselves as we give to our families or to our jobs? Would we be happier?

Some of the most successful people have a strong self-care routine and are aware that the more healthy they are, the more energy they will have to give to their families, their work and their lives. This is true wealth. To care for your mind, body and spirit in an optimal way, is to embody a self-love that can generate an inner happiness that no one can take from you. That's not to say life is devoid of challenges like heartbreak, loss, illness and so on, but when the infrastructure of our lives is solid, we are more prepared to handle the turbulence of life.

Solitude as Loving Self-Care

I think solitude is a big part of self-love. As a Pisces born in the "Week of the Loner," my solitude is my sanctuary. When I am alone, I get to tune into what I am thinking and feeling without the outside noise of other's opinions or judgments. As an artist, my solitude is also a place where I am free to dream and create my visions into reality with the gifts that I have been given.

Some people find it hard to be alone. I think it's important to sit with why that is. I think we should all love and enjoy our own company. If you don't love yourself and your company, then who will? If you don't enjoy being alone, then that can just be an invitation to spend more time with yourself and get more in touch with what brings you peace, comfort, love and joy. The more we are in touch with our needs, then the more easily we can communicate our needs to others' for them to be met.

Self-love requires dedication and discipline. The root word of discipline is "disciple" or student. If self-care is an expression of self-love, then we can become students of ourselves and find joy in discovering what we need to feel healthy, happy and peaceful. We can become like children again and be curious about learning from ourselves while enjoying the journey of life, which itself is a gift.

So often the destination or our goals can change from moment to moment or from season to season so why not just be present and enjoy the ride! To live in gratitude and trusting that life is unfolding perfectly is the faith we need to heal and align with what is best for us.

Two of my favorite writers speak much on solitude and self-love. Rainer Maria Rilke, an Austrian writer who lived over 100 years ago, penned some of the most timeless truths about solitude that deeply resonate with me. From his classic "Letters to a Young Poet," he says, "But your solitude will be a support and a home for you, even in the midst of very unfamiliar circumstances, and from it you will find all your paths" [Ref. 100]. He also says, "Make your ego porous. Will is of little importance, complaining is nothing, fame is nothing. Openness, patience, receptivity, solitude is everything" [Ref. 103].

Renowned writer and professor, bell hooks, wrote extensively on the importance of self-love. My favorite book by her, "All About Love: New Visions," changed my life. Never had I heard someone be so in line with what we all need to hear about this topic. She writes, "When we can see ourselves as we truly are and accept ourselves, we build the necessary foundation for self-love...whether we learn how to love ourselves and others will depend on the presence of a loving environment. Self-love cannot flourish in isolation" [Ref. 104].

Here, hooks expands the notion of self-love from the nest of our solitude moving into a holistic self-love that can only flourish in the presence of a loving community. When I advocate solitude, I am not advocating isolation. We as humans are interconnected and deeply affect each other, so we must cultivate the balance within ourselves and our relationships if we are to live in harmony. We need both the balance of solitude and community to live whole, complete healthy lives. I will explore the importance of community in a later chapter.

What is Love?

When we think of love, what first comes to mind is romantic love, sex and marriage. But I think focusing only on this kind of love is just a fraction of what we can experience from the width and depth of what love can bring into our lives. Being single now for over 10 years, I had to release the societal expectations of "shouldn't you be married by now with kids?"

My answer, "No I shouldn't." I am exactly where I need to be and am content with being free to travel where I want to and do what I want with whom I want when I want. In fact, I think my life is a privilege when my peers and family members who have the traditional life of "married with kids and a 9-5 job" want to be free like me.

In 2022, in the United States alone the marriage industry generated over $61 billion dollars in profits [Ref. 105]. Award-winning financial expert, Romana King says, "Nearly half of American couples go into debt just to get married" [Ref. 106]. According to Divorce and Family lawyers in San Diego, "Almost 50 percent of all marriages in the US will end in divorce or separation [so that's] one divorce every 42 seconds." [Ref. 107]. I will discuss marriage in more detail later, but just some things to consider before rushing into our romanticized idea that marriage is what is best for everyone and that it is something to be done urgently.

Let's be real. Most people marry because they are in love, they have kids together or on the way, because they found someone fine and so on. But what if we treated marriage like a job interview. Beyond those factors, there are other important things to know about someone before getting married. Perhaps, knowing this before marriage could prevent being another statistic that ends in divorce.

Some key things to know about your partner are before getting married: what are their financial habits, their lifestyle choices, values, views on having children or not and how to raise them, religion, where do they want to live, do your families mesh, career goals, how well do you resolve conflict together, non-negotiables and any other specificities that can help alleviate any issues that come up later [Ref. 108].

If you want a long-term relationship, building a connection as friends is a solid foundation rather than just having a connection based on lust and beauty which can run dry after time.

We may overlook other forms of love because of the emphasis society puts on romantic love and marriage. Friendship to me is the most important "-ship." For me, it is the foundation for every healthy relationship. To be healthy friends comes with a mutual understanding and respect for each other's individuality. In codependent romantic partnerships, I find that this sometimes goes out the window and all of the sudden you are owned by someone else and must ask for permission to do and see other people.

This type of love is possessive and jealous which I don't find healthy or appealing, perhaps why I have been happily single. I believe true love is when each person still has their individual freedom to enjoy their lives while still honoring their partnership or what I call interdependence. My best connections whether it be my family, my work partners and in love are all friends or people whom I genuinely love and respect.

All forms of love are important to our health and happiness: self-love, friendships, family connections: of blood and of spirit or chosen family, our pets, work relationships, social community, religious or spiritual community and any encounters we may have, all have value and have something to learn from. Why should we limit ourselves? When in a romantic partnership, I think the energy we gain outside of our relationship will only enhance our love for each other.

Of course, these relationships can only flourish with clear communication based on mutual respect or what I call accountability. Doing what you say and keeping our word or integrity is the basis of trust. What is a relationship without trust? I will dive deeper into the importance of communication in the next chapter.

Our first school for love are our families. Every family has problems. While some of us are fortunate to come from loving families, some families can be dysfunctional and cause us to experience trauma, we need to heal. Then there are some of us who may not even know who their parents were or care to know if they were raised by someone else they love. Spiritual leader and writer, Iyanla Vanzant says "When you inherit a broken family, you can't throw it away and get a new one. What you can do is find people and situations that provide for you what your family cannot."

My chosen family or spirit family a.k.a. non-biological; whether it be my lovers, friends or spiritual community have all been instrumental in helping me heal through toxic behaviors and patterns I learned from my blood family. Adrian Body says "Family isn't just about whose blood runs through your veins. It's about who never left your side, stood up for you and believed in you" [Ref. 110].

What is Intimacy? Love Beyond Sex

In popular media, one would think that love and sex are one in the same. If that were true, more people would be happy. I think love enhances sex. But of course, I would be, being a Pisces. I am a hopeless romantic ruled by my emotions. Sex is a form of communication that can bring about release and wellness. But what if we all believed that was the ultimate expression of love? Then once we had it, we would be completely satisfied?

I want to discuss the importance of intimacy. Intimacy simply means "being close." Being an empath, I love and thrive in intimacy. To have a heart-to-heart conversation and connections with loved ones gives me hope and nourishment to face another day and keep going. Being an empath, I have also been in relation with avoidants and even borderline narcissists who have pushed me away if I got too close to them or expected some type of emotional exchange. I used to be hurt by this but now I feel sorry for them. I don't think avoiding anything is healthy. Open dialogue and processing how we think and feel in a safe space is healthy.

Perhaps, those that avoid intimacy were taught that showing or feeling emotions is a sign of weakness. The "traditional" social model of masculinity is toxic where "men are not supposed to cry or feel" anything but anger. I find American culture to be masculine-dominant where being aggressive and non-emotional is celebrated.

Because of this I see toxic masculinity in both men and women where intimacy is avoided and emotions are to be suppressed. Suppressing anything is unhealthy. Emotions are our internal meter of what is going on with us. Emotions are meant to be experienced then they can be released. By processing or integrating our emotions, or just trying to understand and make sense of them, we can turn our suffering into wisdom. Too often when we stuff our emotions down, then they turn up in toxic ways like addiction, depression, disease or dysfunction in our relationships.

Intimacy is a gift. A mirror in which we can see and experience ourselves, others and love on a deeper level, beyond words, beyond the surface. Now, I must say that not all people are "emotionally safe." I have learned this the hard way. The meter for emotional safe people for me is do they listen well or do they interrupt you when you speak or even worse try to tell you how you should feel. Nope. How do they feel to your nervous system? Do you feel anxious or on-edge? Or do you feel calm around them?

An emotionally safe person will listen to you without judgment, without interruption. They will not make you feel bad for being who you are or what you did. They will accept you and possibly challenge you in a way that can help you grow. I can say I am that type of friend and I am blessed to attract emotionally safe relationships in return. Sometimes, it can be challenging for some folks to find, which is why you can hire a therapist. But even then, you have to build trust since they too start off as strangers.

I recently encountered an excellent and accurate chart of the various types of intimacy we can encounter and nurture in our lives to foster a deeper connection with ourselves and others by therapist and relationship expert, Dr. Elizabeth Fedrick. She breaks down intimacy into 5 areas: emotional, physical, intellectual, spiritual and experiential. She states how intimacy requires effort and attention. Intimacy can only enhance our sexual experiences.

Perhaps, that's where some people fall off because they have the illusion that love is natural and just magically happens without work. bell hooks writes "Love is an action. Never simply a feeling." This is what I call grown-folks love. Perhaps when we were younger, we could be on auto-pilot with love and go through the motions without forethought but as we mature, life becomes complex as do we. So being aware of our motivations, triggers and being accountable for our behavior is what grown love is more about than a fairy tale based on ideas and assumptions. Love is clear, consistent communication. Can you dig it?

Emotional Health as the Foundation for Intimacy

When loving ourselves is not easy neither is fully loving others. It took some long, hard honest looks at myself to understand the ways in which I had been hurt or taught unhealthy ways of loving and was continuing to attract the same patterns that left me feeling unhappy. Emotions get a bad rap in a masculine dominant society as in the United States where I lived the majority of my life. But we all have them, so at some point we have to come to terms with how we feel if we want to heal, no matter what "society" says is acceptable or not.

I came up with the 3 "Emotional I's" which are emotional integration, intelligence and intimacy as a way to understand how to cultivate emotional health. I think there are many ways to achieve emotional health, but here is a tool that I found to be helpful in processing how I feel and gain more control of my emotions and foster emotional health in my relationships. I explored various ways we can experience emotional intimacy in the previous section so I will break down the first two.

The first "I" is emotional integration. We have all been hurt in some way, usually first by our families since for most of us, that is our first school where we learn how to love and relate. The first step and sometimes the hardest step is just acknowledging how we feel. Pain and anxiety is a good indication if something is not good for us. But sometimes we can be in a state of denial about how we really feel or use addictive substances or activities like alcohol, drugs, sex or other things to numb our pain.

Getting in our bodies and being present is essential to feeling our emotions. Many times we are in our heads about our experiences especially if they are traumatic. But if we allow ourselves to fully feel the emotion, the less power it has over us. Emotions can get trapped in our minds and bodies when we hold on to them and can cause illness. Movement helps to process our experiences. I have found success with emotional integration by journaling, meditation, dancing, screaming, kicking objects like cardboard boxes or any vigorous activity that makes us sweat can help to move stuck emotions locked in our minds and bodies.

Whatever the unpleasant emotion, hurt, pain, shame, betrayal, anger, if we set aside time and space to fully experience it in whatever way works for you, then it loses its intensity in our minds. In fact, many spiritual healers believe that all disease originates in the mind or spirit first then manifests in the body. This is why they say if you heal the mind or spirit then the body follows. I believe healing is a holistic process that requires mind, body and spirit integration. So if we are able to engage all three in integrating our emotional experiences, I think we will have the most success.

Fully feeling our emotions helps us to process and integrate them into our experiences. From there, we can have greater clarity on what our emotions are teaching us about what feels good and what does not and make a new informed choice. We are all healers. No one is in your body but you, so listening to how things make you feel is key. Study yourself, there is a wealth of wisdom in your own experiences.

The second "I" is emotional intelligence. Emotional intelligence has two parts, being in tune with how you feel and being able to read how others are feeling through their energy, their words or their body language or what is also known as empathy. Empathy is not an assumption. If you are unsure how your behavior is affecting someone else, just ask. That is the surest way to know, if they are being honest with you of course.

The balance between how you feel and how another feels is important because if we care more for how the other person feels than our own feelings this can cause problems. Vice versa, if we only think of ourselves in a situation then we neglect to consider how our actions may make others feel. Balance is key in all things.

Having emotional intelligence requires listening and observing without judgment. Meditation is a practice I have found most effective in helping me cultivate the non-judgmental observer from within myself. To be able to see my own behavior without a value judgment of good or bad, allows me the space to be objective and just accept myself as I am. Humans are imperfect so we will make mistakes. But a mistake or failure is never wasted, if we learn from it, or "earn" the lesson and use this gained wisdom to make a better choice the next time around.

After we are able to consistently integrate our emotions and develop the practice of being in tune with our own emotions and the emotions of others, then our capacity for emotional intimacy will be easier, deeper and more satisfying. I hope that more people will realize how deeply connected our relationship to our own emotions will allow us more access to a much healthier emotional connection to others.

Monogamy, Marriage, Polyamory and Ways We Partner

Growing up my model for partnership like most people was marriage. My Filipino parents, rest in peace, were devout Catholics and married for over 50 years. Celebrating their Golden anniversary in the Philippines, our native land, with family from all over the world was quite special that I was blessed to be a part of and witness.

Lots of dancing and singing, which my parents were masters at partner dancing: tango, cha-cha, waltz and so on. My father was also a singer where I got my talent from, sang his forever favorite classic "My Way" by Frank Sinatra which was exactly how he led his life. In fact, I sang as well as my sister at the celebration. It was a beautiful milestone.

Their Silver anniversary or 25 years of marriage was also quite a celebration that my sister, rest in peace, organized all the decorations, silver and purple, my Mother's favorite color. She also organized a whole talent show with choreography and costumes with the US Navy in mind, to whom my father served for 30 years. My father in the US Navy and my mother working for the US Embassy, met in their 20s, in Saigon, Vietnam during the war, fell in love and married.

Love in the midst of war is a great way to describe their dynamic. Because no matter what challenges my parents faced, they always worked together as a team. Their devotion and loyalty to each other is the biggest lesson I learned from their marriage.

While monogamy and marriage is the prescribed partnership for most, as I became of age I also learned that they were other forms of partnership that suited different people more. I also observed that monogamy and marriage had its issues that were not always healthy and that marriage was not a prerequisite to have a healthy, happy partnership. Would you believe it if I told you that monogamy was a human creation connected to marriage and Christianity?

For me, I have been in monogamous and polyamorous relationships. Polygamy where you marry multiple people is different from polyamory where you partner with multiple people. I did find that in the end monogamy was easier for me to manage emotionally. But I must admit when I was in a "codependent" monogamous relationship, I longed to be single. Codependency is when two partners lose their individuality and spend all of their time together. I think this model is normalized and partly why I have been single for so long. While being together all the time can be endearing, I also think it is not balanced or healthy.

My heart is happiest when I am free to do what I want with respect to my partner of course. But I found when I was in a codependent relationship, jealousy and possessiveness was normal. An example is being questioned or needing permission when I want to spend time with someone like perhaps an (attractive) friend is met with suspicion and doubt. This is when I realized an interdependent partnership is what I seek where both partners maintain some personal freedom to have their own friends and interests while meeting in the middle respectfully.

For me, a partnership where having respect for each other's individual thoughts, feelings and experiences is paramount to me, instead of melting into one entity. From "Letters to a Young Poet," one of my favorite books by German poet, Rainer Maria Rilke, a quote he wrote that illustrates this interdependent kind of love says "Love consists of this: two solitudes that meet, protect and greet each other" [Ref. 100]. I couldn't agree more.

Masturbation, The Female Orgasm and Sex as Sacred

Something I have noticed is that men and masturbation is a cliché but masturbation and women is taboo. Why is that?

Maybe because sex is defined as "penetration" and considered done when the man orgasms. I am generalizing but you see this type of sex modeled in films, TV and even in pornography. From this perspective, male pleasure is prioritized over a female's orgasm, which usually takes longer to achieve.

According to a study done by the Archives of Sexual Behavior, "Heterosexual women have fewer orgasms than men or lesbian or bisexual women" or what is called the "orgasm gap" (Ref. 193). The study was conducted with 52,600 people in the U.S. across genders and sexual orientations (Ref. 193).

I remember watching an independent film called "Shortbus" where this middle-aged Asian woman and her boyfriend are having loud, aggressive sex throughout the film. Then towards the end of the film, she admits that she has never experienced an orgasm.

I think there are several reasons why this is common. I don't think enough women are encouraged to explore and know their own bodies and what gives them sexual pleasure. Instead, some heterosexual women are waiting for a "man" to "find" it for them. Some may get lucky, while statistics show many do not.

I support knowing what gives our bodies' sexual pleasure through masturbation. Because once you know what you like, then you can communicate to your lover what gets you off. It is an act of self-love. To be in touch with what gives you pleasure is key to having regular orgasms.

I discovered what an orgasm was when I was around ten years old after finding a vibrator, my mother used for massage. It was an exhilarating pleasure that eased my mind and relaxed my body. I loved it. I discovered that my body was able to have multiple orgasms in one session.

Why is this taboo? I want to be part of the female orgasm revolution encouraging women at any age to get to learn what pleases their bodies sexually. Because once you know this, you won't "need" anyone to achieve an orgasm. And when you are having sex with someone, your self-knowledge will only enhance your experience.

As a female, I also think foreplay such as intimacy, kissing, talking dirty, asking for what you want, sharing sexual fantasies, kink, massage, touching a woman's clitoris, oral sex or what old school people call "kindling" the fire are essential in helping women achieve orgasms. If a man is ready to penetrate a woman and her vagina isn't even wet, that says a lot about how much he cares about her sexual experience.

"Few heterosexual women climax through penetrative sex alone" says the study above (Ref. 193). I think many hetero men believe that penetrative sex is enough for women to orgasm. But from this study it's clear that the female is not aroused enough for her to get there.

As a lesbian, being fully aroused or "wet" is a prerequisite to having a female orgasm myself or giving one to my partner. The wetter, the better. The clitoris is a very important organ, arousing a woman to orgasm. The clitoris to a woman is the equivalent to a man's penis, containing more than "10,000 nerve endings that create sexual pleasure (Ref. 194).

Sadly, some hetero men do not even know where the clitoris is. From watching porn, they don't know how to touch it properly. The clit, for short, is a delicate organ that does not need a lot of pressure to be stimulated. A light, gentle touch can make a woman fully aroused. If a man is in tune with a woman, he will want to bring her to full arousal for them both to have a better experience. And if a woman has already explored her own clit and what brings her pleasure, then she will know and teach a man if he does not know how to please her properly. Communication is key.

There are also different kinds of orgasms to explore in females: clitoral, vaginal, G-spot and multiple. Tantra suggests there is even a nipple-gasm whereby breast stimulation alone can bring a female to orgasm.

Now that I am older, I am less driven by lust and passion. I seek a deeper connection with those I share my body with. Having a mental and emotional connection with someone is a prerequisite to being sexually intimate. In this way, we can bring back the sacred to sex.

Sex can be a very spiritual experience especially if it is with someone you love. If you have a one night stand, you are opening your body to someone you know nothing about which can be risky on various levels.

A study shows that only 1 in 10 women will orgasm from a one-night stand while 64% of men will achieve orgasm in the same instance (Ref. 195). A stranger doesn't know what you like and alcohol may be involved which can lower the possibility of achieving orgasm.

I now see sex as an expression of love. For me, knowing and loving the person I am engaging in a sexual connection with only enhances my experience and deepens our bond together.

What stage you are in life and what your needs are will dictate, with whom and why you have sex. In any case, knowing your body, what pleases you and knowing the person you are engaging sexually with can only create a better experience for you.

Chapter 6: Reflections:
How can you incorporate more daily self-loving activities?

Chapter 7

Communication: Relating, Involving, Resolving, Evolving

Communication is the basis for everything. To commune means to be in close contact with another. And if how we do anything is how we do everything, then our relationship with ourselves reflects how well we relate to others.

Yes, there are challenges in society like oppression and poverty, that are out of our control, which can cause strain in a relationship. But I also believe the source of the suffering we face in our relationships is rooted in our own suffering. That is why mental health and self-care is key to maintaining balance in this stressful modern-day world.

If we don't do the work to maintain inner peace, how do we expect to have outer balance and harmony with others? It took me a long time to realize this. However, the work to maintain inner peace is never done, it's a daily practice to choose to be happy.

Our environment can contribute to our wellness or unhappiness as well which is also something to be aware of. At this point in my life, I have moved out of big US cities where I lived for over 20 years and am now fortunate to live as a digital nomad in mostly tropical places.

I currently live in Playa Del Carmen, Mexico which has about half a million people and the centerpiece is the beach. My first time living in the tropics in my life. As a Filipino, my homeland is the Philippines which is the largest archipelago (group of islands) in the world. I feel so at home now. My spirit feels at peace by the water and in warm weather all year round. This has greatly improved my mood. Making a conscious choice of where you live will greatly impact your mental health, and the type of community you attract.

Relating is More Than What We Say

The foundation of any healthy relationship is communication. Communication is more than what we say but also how we say it. Studies show that 70-90 % of our communication is expressed through our body language. Our energy or vibration conveys information, saying a lot about people and their intentions. I am particularly sensitive to the frequency of people's vibrations and can feel bad vibes or if someone is not being completely honest with me.

We all have intuition, that inner voice that speaks to us when something is off or right on about someone. How tuned in we are to our inner voice is another issue but it's there. How do we explain why we choose to go down one street versus another or stop at this store over another and end up running into someone we know? I believe this is the spirit world at work, always guiding us whether we recognize it or not. Is this a random coincidence or synchronicity?

Synchronicity, defined by renowned Swiss psychiatrist Carl Jung is a "psychologically meaningful connection between an inner event (e.g., thought, image, dream) and one or more external events occurring simultaneously" (Ref. 129). I am a firm believer in synchronicity and the power of our thoughts or vibrations to attract what we think. I am no longer surprised when I make new friends or run into old friends when I am traveling across the world or walking around in my neighborhood. The law of attraction is a fact of nature.

This is why I meditate to guard my mind from negative thoughts and have transformed many fear-based perceptions. As Buddhism states, the mind is reality. I am human so I do have a tendency to have negative thoughts, but I notice when I am in a bad mood I attract negative experiences. Keeping my garden free of "weeds" or bad thoughts, is how I can control my experiences. We can't always foresee what challenges come our way but our relationship with ourselves, our inner speech, our perspective and our attitude can determine the types of experiences and people we attract.

I think healthy communication starts with the relationship we have with ourselves. Do you have a negative person in your life who is always causing you stress? Some of my family members were "negative Nellies" and I can only imagine how toxic their inner speech was. I found it to be peaceful and comforting to be around my kin who were calm and positive. This is how interconnected we are to each other and how connected our thoughts are to our state of being.

Authenticity as the Starting Point for World Peace

To me, listening is more important than speaking when relating to others. I love to talk about things I am passionate about, but deeply listening to others when they speak rather than waiting for your turn to speak is what learning from each other is all about.

We are all here doing our best. Communication is the key that determines how well we will relate to each other. Being fully present, mindfully listening to each other so we can respond in kind is what makes us human. When we dominate a conversation, we miss the dynamic authentic exchange that happens when we give others space to speak.

As a teacher and speaker, I know my power to use my words to express myself in a group. But I stop myself in a group, I stop to engage others by asking questions. Everyone has something to teach and something to learn. When we come from awareness and respect for humanity, we can cultivate more authentic connections with others and build community wherever we are in this world.

Being curious about other people's experiences is key to having a global citizen perspective. Learning from those who are different from us—builds empathy for each other's struggles and circumstances.

Art is a big part of humanity that unites us. Just consider the impact of music, like the work of legendary US artist like Michael Jackson. His album, "Thriller," sold over 70 million copies worldwide. Most of these countries where it sold do not speak English, but that didn't stop people from feeling the authenticity of the music and relating to his message.

No one exists in a silo. We affect each other whether we recognize it or not. Living authentically—by living the truth of who we are—can only inspire others to do the same. If we all had reverence for people beyond identity, national and political lines, could world peace be more possible? World peace starts within us, our communities, then ripples out globally. Our impact is that powerful.

Involving: What Our Relationships Require of Us

Once someone becomes more than an acquaintance to us, we have a responsibility to maintain a healthy connection. Respectful communication and clearly communicated boundaries are paramount. Without respect, there is no relationship. This is why I am so centered on friendship. Friendship is the basis of every happy relationship. I find that friendship enhances all my relationships—whether romantic, work or family, with genuine mutual caring.

In healthy friendships, there is a natural balance where harmony and connection happens with grace and ease. Typically, there is no possession—you are free to come and go as you please without this feeling of obligation. I was once in a romantic partnership that became toxic. I had to worry about my partner becoming jealous or upset if I did something without them. When there is too much control and restriction in a relationship, resentment will arise and ultimately create conflict if not addressed and resolved.

Co-dependence, or becoming too enmeshed in someone else's behavior, is not healthy. Interdependence, where each person is free to pursue their own passions can only enhance a healthy relationship. Being with the same person all the time is not only unhealthy, but it's just boring. It's great to have a life partner or best friend, but maintaining other healthy connections is important for balance.

When two people support each other's lives while nurturing their connection, relationships flourish. Having respect for each other requires us to love and accept people for who they are, not who we want them to be. This is why my chosen family is so important to me. Because even though my blood family may have different lifestyles and values than I do, my chosen family—friends who become family—are people who love me as I am, share common interests and respect the unique value I bring to the world. Acceptance from your community is essential to happiness.

With Freedom Comes Boundaries

In romantic partnerships, having freedom and clearly communicated boundaries is key to having a healthy balance. For instance, in a monogamous relationship, your partner should be free to have their own friends but not sleep with other people. Being romantic with one person in a monogamous relationship is a boundary that must be respected. If not, that's cheating.

In a polyamorous relationship, each person is free to see other people romantically. When I was polyamorous with a woman, we agreed that we would communicate who the new person first was before we got involved with someone outside of our primary relationship. Clearly communicating boundaries and sticking to our energetic contracts we agreed to helps reduce conflict and hurt feelings.

When an inevitable conflict occurs, we must work to resolve them directly and not ignore or deny that it exists. Doing this only adds insult to injury and just feels fake. If I find myself with someone, who is unwilling to resolve conflict, I quickly move on because avoidance is not my value. Self-awareness requires emotional maturity so we can choose what we will accept and what we will not.

Resolving: Self-Awareness, Compassion and Courage Required

Conflict is part and parcel of being human. Where are we taught how to resolve conflict? When I was growing up, "resolving conflict" meant becoming angry, arguing, blaming and sometimes becoming violent. This is why I struggled with cultivating healthy relationships especially when I entered my first romantic relationships.

Once I started practicing Nichiren Buddhism in my late 20s, I was introduced to the notion that "dialogue is a form of peace and the answer to war." Meaning, the only way we can resolve conflict is if we talk to each other. Sounds simple, right?

It can be. However, before conflict can be resolved through dialogue, certain elements need to be in place. First, each person must be self-aware about what caused the conflict. Usually, conflict is caused by misunderstanding. When we communicate on sensitive topics that trigger our emotions, we must navigate carefully with compassion. If the conflict is intense, taking time to calm down, reflect on our reaction and come back to our rational mind before communicating again is essential.

We often communicate or argue from a place of hurt and say awful things to each other, which only escalates and complicates the conflict. Some couples develop a "safe word" for when one is triggered by a known issue so that they can refrain from escalating and revisit it later. However, this is only a temporary fix. At some point, the conflict must be addressed and resolved together.

If the conflict is not resolved, it will usually resurface as passive aggressive behavior. Some examples of this are: "ghosting" or being unresponsive, making a back-handed compliment, being uncooperative and delaying when you ask them to do something, giving you excuses rather than being direct about how they feel, giving you the silent treatment and gaslighting.

In the past, when in a conflict with someone that gave me silent treatment, I would allow it. But after realizing that I deserve respect, I now recognize this as toxic behavior that must be addressed and resolved. If they continue to avoid conflict, that is a red flag that I do not need to be in relation with this person.

Gaslighting is when someone does something wrong to you, then they deny that it happened. They may do this by deflecting a conversation or twisting a situation to make you feel crazy, or that you imagined it happened. Either way, it's a red flag that this is a toxic relationship that does not deserve your time and energy.

When we communicate, there are layers to what is being said and what is understood by the listener. This is where misunderstandings can begin. But with self-awareness and the desire to understand each other without blame or needing to be "right," we can begin to dialogue and expose the deeper layers of what is going on.

Compassion is essential in conflict resolution. We can only move through conflict with empathy and understanding for each other's perspective and experience. A self-care routine with daily meditation really helps us to become more aware of how we feel inside and have self-compassion. Then we can begin to develop compassion and the courage to care for others. Our behavior towards ourselves is a mirror for how we will treat others.

Meditation and self-reflection is essential for me in cultivating healthy relationships. Healthy does not mean without conflict. It means that when conflict does arise, both people are willing to work together respectfully to resolve it. Communication is not a perfect system but a willingness to work on ourselves and acquire new ways of communicating during conflict is best.

Courage is required to face conflict head on with face-to-face dialogue. Yes, it can create feelings of anxiety when something uncomfortable has happened between you and someone else. But ignoring conflict is a function of the ego and will only breed resentment in the long run. To stay in the ignorance of your own assumptions of what someone else thinks and project what you feel onto the situation is not reality. This is what happens when we choose not to talk to each other. It's not healthy.

The reality is that everyone experiences the same situations differently. Our perception is colored by our identity, our experiences, our feelings and our level of self-awareness. When we are in conflict with someone, these factors will differ between people. That's why it is important for us to talk when we are in conflict with someone, to gain clarity and understanding.

If a conflict has triggered a deeper issue or trauma that someone has not done the self-work to understand and heal, then seeking therapy, entheogenic healing or outside emotional support that is safe is necessary to heal deeper layers of our subconscious mind.

My older sister, may she rest in peace, was someone who endured multiple traumas early in her life. She did not transform them in healthy ways but used addictions to food and shopping to sublimate her pain. Sublimating traumas with addictions is only a temporary external fix and will never heal the root of our inner trauma. Because of this, a simple conversation with her could trigger anger and defensiveness. We all know someone like this, and perhaps sometimes this person is us.

The human experience of enduring trauma is universal. The difference is what we choose to do about it. Being mentally healthy is a choice. First, you must choose to believe you have the power to change your mind and rewrite your story to heal, rather than staying a victim to your past and repeating toxic patterns that keep you unhappy.

This is why self-work is so important in having healthy communication and healthy relationships. Being committed to understanding ourselves reflects how well others will understand us. Now in my 40s, I pride myself in knowing who I am as opposed to my 20s when I was still figuring out who I was.

Maturity isn't just about age but it comes from life experiences and the willingness to learn from them. Some people mature early on while some older people never do. There is always room to learn and grow no matter your age. I do not compare my growth to others but only measure my growth by becoming a better person than I was yesterday.

Tools for Creating Safety in Resolving Conflict:

Nonviolent Communication (NVC)

Relationships are the crux of our existence, so learning how to resolve conflict is paramount in having a happy life. If dialogue is the bridge to understanding, how do we make sure it's done fairly and respectfully?

When I ran an elementary after-school program at a charter school in Oakland, California, I first encountered non-violent communication or NVC. It was required that all staff be trained to use and teach this to our students. Non-violent communication addresses the errors of miscommunication in the language of blame and judgment that feed an unending cycle of conflict.

Non-violent communication is based on the principle of non-violence (related to Buddhism) and was developed by clinical psychologist Marshall Rosenberg in the 1960s-70s, as a means "to build empathy and improve the quality of life for people."

The premise of non-violent communication has four parts: observation, feelings, needs and requests. It is a tool that can be applied individually, within a relationship or within a group and works as follows:

Observations:
1) What I observe: see, remember, imagine, free from my assumptions that do or do not contribute to my well-being
- *Address by saying "When I see…"*

Feelings:
2) How I feel: emotion or sensation, rather than thought in relation to what I observe
- *Address by saying "I feel…"*

Needs:
3) What I need or value rather than a preferences that causes my feelings
- *Address by saying "…because I need/value…"*

Requests:
4) The concrete action I would like to be taken
- *Address by saying "Would you be willing to…"*

In short, the format of NVC goes, *"When I see…I feel…because I need…Would you be willing to…?"*

For example, if I was having a conflict with my lover being possessive over me hanging out with other women. I would say, "When I see you becoming jealous whenever my friend Tania comes to hang, I feel uncomfortable, like it's a crime for me to have friends because I need to have relationships outside of ours to be healthy. Would you be willing to control your emotions and work on your own trust issues?"

When we approach a conflict with this wording versus from a place of blame and judgment like "You really piss me off when you act like a jealous b**ch." This is typically how people behave when we react quickly instead of responding thoughtfully. It's really a matter of maturity and whether we are willing to slow down our emotions and choose to create value rather than conflict. It will take some retraining and practice but it is worth trying if we want to have more health and harmony in our relationships.

Satyagraha: "Holding on to Truth"

Spiritual and political leader, Mahatma Gandhi, was known for his effective nonviolent civil disobedience campaigns to gain India's independence from British colonial rule. His nonviolent approach to resolving conflict inspired Dr. Martin Luther King, Jr., Nelson Mandela, Albert Einstein and more.

Satyagraha or "holding on to truth" is a nonviolent means of resolving conflict he developed. It was used in many social movements to affirm the human rights of oppressed people around the world. The method is that for example, if two people, Tim and Alexa, are having a conflict, both will have their own ideas and experiences.

Let's say Tim's ideas and experiences are A and B and Alexa's experiences are B and C. Part one is to first acknowledge and identify Tim's A and Alexa's C. This is where each person has their own unique perception of the situation or where they differ. Then part two is to acknowledge B where both people are in agreement. It is from point B, or where both people have resonance and can build from that place moving forward.

The intention behind Gandhi's philosophy of nonviolence is to conquer hatred with love, anger with humility, selfishness with sacrifice and a willingness to find common ground. Satyagraha is a method to build cooperation and maintain harmony even when there is a difference in experience or value.

Circle Communication

In my long residence of living in the progressive San Francisco Bay area, I was involved in numerous nonprofits and attended community meetings that used the ancient practice of circle communication. Circle communication was used in rituals, initiations, rites of passage and celebrations in indigenous communities like Native American and African cultures. Sitting in a circle to communicate represents the connection we share to each other and to all things, helping to build unity within a group.

Circle communication can be used in any situation to create community, run a staff meeting or professional development for a business, teach a workshop, to process grief, to resolve conflict or any matter of concern where unity and safety is desired. Also known as circling, it is a container where the individual contributes while building solidarity based on the mutual values of a group.

For example, Alcoholics Anonymous meetings and other support groups use circle communication. Inspired by Christianity, Quakers believe that God is love and that each person has this love and inner light within them and can access God on their own. Quakers sit in a circle when in worship to see each other and establish equality. Quakers believe in the equal rights of humans and allow women the space to speak in public meetings.

When I sat in circles in an organization, we first established ground rules or agreements on how we will communicate to be respectful of each other. Some common agreements among these are: speaking from "I" statements as found in NVC (nonviolent communication), the term "one mic" or only one person speaks at a time or physically using a talking stone which means the same, when one person is speaking they are given to space to speak fully until done without any interruption.

You can also establish an exercise to open the circle such as appreciation where each person expresses what they appreciate about the group or someone in it. It could even be an appreciation for oneself if the focus is self-love. This can set the tone for a positive dialogue. You can also assign a closing exercise or ritual like declarations or statements on what actions you will take to improve yourself or a situation or simply stating what you learned from the activity.

These tools for circle communication can be used in a dyad or that is a dialogue between two people to build a safe container to resolve issues as well as within a group. When I was in a relationship, my partner and I used these tools if we came into a conflict. It really helps, especially if you are in a relationship where you don't "fight fairly." It takes mindfulness, intention and patience to integrate these tools into your relationship but it is worth a try if you have recurring conflicts that need to be resolved.

Restorative Justice

Within the US legal system resolving crime is dealt with by some form of punishment. In this model of justice based on retribution, the offenders must be punished like going to jail. It is debatable whether those imprisoned for their crimes are reformed and rehabilitated by the system.

In the 1970s, American criminologist Howard Zehr developed an alternative resolution to crime called restorative justice. Restorative justice views crimes and misconduct as violations of people and harm to the community. It is a set of practices that create a safe container for a dialogue or circle communication between those affected to come together to seek resolution.

While retributive justice is offender-focused, in restorative justice, space is given to the victim, their family or community members, the offender and in some cases justice and legal personnel, to speak respectfully and seek healing together. It encourages empathy, collaboration and input from all impacted parties to create a positive outcome from what has happened. By accessing the wisdom in each voice, each experience, a stronger community is created. It is a model that seeks to humanize and positively transform the way in which the traditional US legal system deals with crime.

Evolving: Growing Together Over Time

All relationships go through changes, stages and challenges. But how can we sustain relationships over time? In the beginning of a relationship, it's easy to romanticize who they are and relish the newness and dopamine rush. But what happens when you come out of the honeymoon phase?

According to neuroscientists, Helen Fisher and Lucy Brown, relationships go through four stages (Ref. 128)

- **Stage 1: The euphoric stage** - 6 months - 2 years
- **Stage 2: The early attachment stage** - 1-5 years
- **Stage 3: The crisis stage** - 5-7 years
- **Stage 4: The deep attachment stage** - 7 years & beyond

In the euphoric stage, you idealize our partner. Their imperfections are cute and mistakes are easily forgiven. According to Fisher and Brown in this stage, there is a decrease in activity of the brain where negative judgment occurs. They propose that the longer the couple can sustain negative judgment the longer they will be together.

When I was in a long-term committed relationship, around the two year mark, we had to confront issues that would determine whether our relationship would endure. Once the euphoria wears off, your partner becomes more familiar and you identify more with them. In this stage, Fisher and Brown say that you will be able to sleep and not obsess about each other.

During the crisis stage around the 5-7 year mark is the make it or break it point where they say couples can drift apart. I think a crisis could strike a relationship at any point. But in any relationship, whether you can move through conflict with someone else will depend on the quality of your communication and conflict resolution skills.

After this stage, if you can successfully overcome conflict, you develop a deeper attachment and there is a calm, security to your relationship. I have felt this develop in friendships I have had over 10 years where we have seen each other through different stages of life and moved through conflict so our bond is stronger. These evolutionary stages of a relationship help us understand how the brain works.

In the end, both people must be committed to growing together and practice effective conflict resolution skills to maintain respectful communication and weather the test of time. Having shared passions and common values is essential because even if people change, these points of connection that can help sustain a relationship over time.

Since needs can change over time, communicating often what our needs are in a relationship will ultimately help keep clarity.

Sometimes, there are differences between people that cannot be resolved. It may be a sign to let go and move on. I believe in the power of not forcing things especially if you have repeatedly tried and failed to restore balance for a considerable time. I recognize the abundance of the universe and in those instances moving forward can be just what is needed to attract a new relationship that will serve us better and reflect what we need.

***Chapter 7: Reflections*:**
What conflict resolution tools can you use to improve your relationships?

Chapter 8

Community: Being in Alignment, Finding Support, Being of Service in Our Purpose and Mentorship

Community is vital to every species on our planet. It is the system in which living things work together to create support so that its inhabitants' needs are met. Community provides social connection and a sense of belonging which is vital to our happiness, mental health and being able to find what we need to survive.

Our family is the first community we belong to, then our schools, religious or spiritual community, our work community and more.

From ancient to modern times, community is where we share important milestones to honor and celebrate our lives. We mark rites of passage for youth including sweet sixteen parties, Jewish bar/bat mitzvah, Latin quinceaneras and in Filipino culture, it's called it a "debut." Ceremonial events like graduations, birthdays, anniversaries, weddings and funerals within a community shape who we are.

Having communities witness our passage through the turning points of life is vital to forming our identity and shaping how we relate to the world. Circle communication or sitting in a circle dialogue is very healing. Rituals like grief circles or addiction recovery meetings such as Alcoholics Anonymous, both use circle communication to be seen and heard which is vital to healing.

Writer Iyanla Vanzant said, "When you stand and share your story in an empowering way, your story will heal you and your story will heal somebody else." It's powerful to share our truth in a safe space where we are seen and heard. I know this from being an artist. When I perform a poem, song, DJ set, share a photo or just dance at the club, people come up and show me love for inspiring them.

To "inspire" comes from the Latin root word, "breath" or "to impart a truth upon someone." Sharing art in a community is an incredible source of healing and inspiration that I find vital to my well-being. Community is a place of learning and human connection that gives life meaning and cohesion.

Murri artist and activist, Lilla Watson said, "If you have come to help me, you are wasting your time. But if you have come because your liberation is tied up with mine, then let us work together." This is the work, to realize that we are all connected. When we heal and love ourselves enough to show up, to be seen and to be heard, we give others permission to do the same. To feel the love and support of our community is vital to our collective healing and liberation.

Being in Alignment and Living with Authenticity

Being in alignment in spirituality means to be in harmony with yourself in mind, body and spirit. When you live in alignment, you live from a place of authenticity or in a lane that is uniquely your own. Living true to who you are requires self-work.

Our passions can reveal our purpose. Doing the work of understanding your values, passions, strengths and weaknesses will reflect in the quality of your life. To know myself and to live from my truth with the desire to constantly grow and improve myself, is happiness. This happiness does not live outside of you, it comes from self-reflection, self-awareness and self-discovery. What a gift to know oneself, my solitude is my sanctuary.

Self-growth is not about perfection, it's about progress. Competition can fuel your drive and passion to succeed, but the best growth is when it's grounded in yourself. If you are better today than you were yesterday, that's a success!

Authenticity does not lie in comparing yourself to another's path. Progress and success will look different for everyone. Accepting this will save you from a lot of suffering and not trying to be like anyone but yourself.

It's a success when you live your life according to your own path, even if it means walking alone. When we live authentically from what we believe to be true, we live with integrity. Integrity is when your beliefs, words and actions are in agreement. By living in alignment, we send a clear message to the universe of what we desire. Therefore, manifestation and attracting support becomes as natural as breathing.

How Do We Come into Alignment?

This book is about coming into alignment. Returning to our essence, our natural state of love, health and abundance is the work of alignment. Each chapter is devoted to some aspect of ourselves or our lives that need our awareness, attention and loving care. When we are inwardly focused on loving ourselves, this quality will be reflected in our behavior and the universe will reflect more of this energy to us.

We teach others how to treat us by the way we treat ourselves. If you constantly speak negatively about yourself—inside your head or out loud, chances are that you will attract others who confirm your negative ideas about yourself.

Positive self-talk, having a regular self-care routine and spending time with those who encourage and empower you will bring more alignment into your life. When we take great care of ourselves, we will attract people who confirm the way we value ourselves. When we are at our best, then we can show and care for others in a way that's healthy and sustainable. It's all interconnected.

Being in nature brings us in alignment with the natural rhythms of the elements and brings you into deeper alignment with yourself. When you are in this state of mind, finding people who share common interests and values, will come with greater ease and grace. You may need to do some research to find a supportive community, but just going out into the world with faith and positivity can also attract some of the best, most unexpected magical connections.

Meditation is a powerful alignment practice. Meditation helps us to be more grounded and centered in who we are and why we are here. By developing a deeper state of self-awareness, you feel more comfortable asking deeper questions to understand yourself, and this gives you a greater capacity to understand others.

Lao Tzu, founder of Taoism and the I Ching, said, "Knowing others is intelligence; knowing yourself is true wisdom. Mastering others is strength; mastering yourself is true power."

When I am grounded and centered in who I am, I am less concerned about appearances and what others think of me and more engaged with the truth of what I am experiencing in the moment.

Even in the face of the "prescribed reality" of what society wants you to believe, which could be making you ill and unhappy, if you are able to listen deeply to your own truth, then you can find a path that is in more alignment with what can bring you health and happiness.

In his book "The Seat of the Soul," Gary Zukav likens karma to the third law of motion in physics which is "for every action, there is an equal and opposite reaction." Knowing this can help us understand just how powerful we are in creating our reality. By taking responsibility for our vibration or energy, we can intentionally choose what we want to experience at any given moment.

The best-selling book, "The Secret" by Rhonda Byrne, is a staple on the power of the law of attraction. The Buddhist adage, "mind is reality" embodies this law. Henry Ford's take on this principle when he said "Whether you think you can, or you think you can't – you're right."

Our thoughts, words and actions create our lives. If we accept this, then we are no longer a victim to our circumstances. We are an active agent, choosing the experiences we will have. A key part of being in our center and in alignment is being present.

In his best-selling book, "The Power of Now" by Eckhart Tolle, he said, "Realize deeply that the present moment is all you have. Make the NOW the primary focus of your life." When we are fully present, we are not depressed about our past nor are we anxious about our future. Living in the moment becomes simple, like the child on the street dancing to the rhythm of their spirit. How beautiful to be in this fully embodied state?

Finding peace by living fully in the moment in our bodies also means to release the busy mind and our thoughts. Often, our minds will make assumptions about what other people are thinking or experiencing. This can cause us to suffer but we do not know what others are experiencing unless we ask them. Dialogue can bridge any confusion if people are willing to communicate respectfully.

Eckhart Tolle wrote "The primary cause of unhappiness is never the situation but your thoughts about it." We must decide where our power lies. Is it outside of us or within? To consciously choose our thoughts, words and actions to create the life we envision for ourselves is true alignment.

Alignment or returning to our natural state can be likened to when we are children. The other day I saw a child have a great time just dancing up and down the sidewalk with no music. Joy and play is our natural state.

Love and connection is a human need we all share. Let us take the time to love and connect with ourselves first by starting our morning with meditation, journaling or anything that helps us self-reflect and fill our minds with positivity and peace.

When we do, this love will ripple out to our relationships and our communities. By cultivating harmony and balance within ourselves, this alignment will be undeniable in our lives.

How Do You Know You Are in Alignment?

When you are in alignment, you know who you are and what your purpose is. Taking the time to understand this about yourself, is the work.

When you are in alignment, you attract what you need when you need it. Synchronicity is normal. For instance, as you are saying something the universe brings it to you or sends you a sign that your thought is attracting the reality you hold in your mind's eye. We are powerful magnets so being clear about what we want and holding that vision in our minds is key in manifesting our desires.

Barbadian artist and mystic Neville Goddard, coined the philosophy and practice called the law of assumption, which states that "by believing the thing you want already exists in your life, you'll manifest it into existence." Starting from the assumption that our desires are already real, brings them into manifestation faster because it exists within us first. When you are a vibrational match for the thing you are desiring, then it will magnetize to you.

The opposite is also true. If you desire an outcome, but do not truly believe it or do not take action to realize it, then you are sending a mixed message to the universe. Self-contradiction is commonly why manifestation does not happen. An honest evaluation of where you focus your energy to manifest your desire, is key in coming into alignment with what you want.

Magnetism has to do with your mental and emotional state with the body and spirit influencing both. When we are healthy in our body and peaceful in our spirit then feeling joy and wellness comes more easily. Being in a positive, loving or even passionate state of mind is highly magnetic. Others are drawn to you, especially children and animals.

How do I know this? Synchronicity is a sign of alignment that we are all connected. Wherever I go, I run into someone I know from the other side of the world or down the street. And whenever I travel, I always find like-minded friends. This was modeled to me as a child when I saw my parents connect to "strangers" and build community with grace and ease.

First of all, I want to say that not all "strangers" are safe. As an intuitive I can sense vibration and if I get an ill or negative vibe, I do not align with that person, I draw a boundary.

Most times wherever I roam in this beautiful world, I find the most kind, beautiful people from all walks of life, ages and ethnicities. My nickname is Univibes, because I truly believe that there is a "universal vibration" or Univibes for short, that connects all people, all life. Because of this belief, I have built a global tribe, both virtually and in real life.

When we are vibrating high or magnetically aligned with our purpose, anything goes in this magical state of limitless possibilities.

It didn't occur to me how aligned my life was until I became older. When I started to meditate regularly, I became more aware of it, because the synchronicities became stronger and more frequent. Now I embrace my alignment as the result of living authentically.

My thoughts, words and actions are aligned with the beliefs I hold about myself. I attract a community wherever I go and this determines the kinds of experiences I have. I only manifest amazing experiences, because I believe I am awesome!!

What do you believe about yourself? Is it time to rewrite your story? Is it a sad story or a love story? Are you the hero or the victim? You are your life's writer, director and actor. What do you want to create? Make it happen, captain.

Finding Community is a Result of Being in Alignment

My parents were aligned people. They traveled to over 42 countries in their lives while my Dad worked for the US Navy and my Mom worked for the US Philippine Embassy mostly during the lives of my sister and brother who are older than me.

When we settled in the DMV area (Washington D.C., Southern Maryland, Northern Virginia), I traveled with them locally and abroad and we would always run into someone they knew or other Filipinos. My parents, even if they didn't know them, would just start talking to them.

Through them, I learned the importance of building community wherever I go in the world, and especially locally within the community where I live. While growing up, my parents were also leaders in several Filipino organizations and religious groups, often planning, leading and hosting big events, prayer groups and regular socials.

Because of this, my parents had an active social life and many friends in the community to share with in fellowship. I also had a large extended family in the DMV area that also was a big support growing up—lots of cousins, aunties, uncles and grandparents to share in family milestones and gatherings.

My parents lived to be in their eighties. I believe their devotion to their family, faith and spirituality as well as having a sense of belonging to their various communities contributed to their longevity.

Based in Oakland, California, as a spiritual leader for over 10 years with my Nichiren Buddhist organization, SGI-USA, my understanding of community deepened. SGI-USA is the most humanistic modern-day religion I have found to date.

My role as a leader was to pray with and teach others about Buddhist teachings. Showing them how to pray using the chanting meditation of reciting "Nam myoho renge kyo" as a tool to overcome obstacles and seeing them have "actual proof" or their prayers answered, was deeply fulfilling. This gave me an incredible sense of purpose and a deeper confidence. By helping others, we in turn expand our own lives.

With SGI-USA, I learned what human equality and the unconditional support of a community felt like. I was able to be seen, heard and appreciated for my entire identity as a queer, Filipino female artist and teacher. I was also able to host, emcee and sing at member meetings by sharing my skills and talent to contribute to the community.

In our smaller meetings, we sat in circles so everyone could see each other and had a chance to share their stories. In our larger meetings, we would pray together then listen to stories of community members using the practice of chanting to transform their lives, turning poison into medicine, transforming obstacles into benefit and winning in their life.

I am forever grateful for this community. SGI or Soka-Gakkai International, a Japanese form of Buddhism, is based in over 192 countries and territories. When I traveled to Amsterdam, I was able to chant and share meals with some Buddhist elder expats who treated me like family.

Ultimately, it's up to you to forge community connections whether it's through your family, your work, your spiritual community or by finding others who share your passions or values. Finding community becomes natural as breathing when you are in alignment.

Recognizing and Honoring Our Global Interconnectedness

We can look to the indigenous people of the Earth for many of the solutions to our modern day problems. They lived in harmony with the Earth and the natural cycles so they were in tune and aligned with universal laws that stand the test of time.

There are many concepts from indigenous wisdom that resonate with my belief in "Univibes" which is my musical alias. My name represents the need for unity across all borders and boundaries to heal ourselves and our planet. This is the reason I am writing this book, for world peace starting with ourselves. My life path number is also the number 1 which represents leadership, independence and pioneering.

There is a song by one of my favorite house DJ/producers Atjazz and Glass Slipper, who made a song called "Unification Vibration." The lyrics say " How can you end your suffering? If you don't know that we are one. We've been around forever. We're meant to grow together. This is my house, your house. Our only house."

When I encountered this song, I realized the deeper meaning behind my musical name, Univibes. The message of "Unification Vibration" is about how we need to live responsibly because we affect one another. This is exactly aligned with what I believe. What a gift when we find in our lives a reflection of what we believe. That is alignment.

The Australian indigenous people, the Aborigines, believe in "kanyini," the idea that there is a sacred connectedness between all humanity and that we must all take responsibility and have unconditional love for all of creation.

The African indigenous Zulu tribe believes in "ubuntu" meaning "I am because we are." They believe there is a universal bond that connects all humanity. This is very similar to the indigenous Mayan code of the heart, "In Lak'ech Ala K'in" which means "I am you, you are me."

These universal principles directly inform the modern-day term "global interconnectedness." Global interconnectedness is "the ability to function in an increasingly multicultural, international, yet interconnected environment. It fosters the development of individuals to become successful professionals, civic leaders, and informed citizens in a diverse national and global society" [Ref. 25].

If our leaders based our social systems on these modern philosophies informed by indigenous values, we could ensure the safety of future generations by protecting our planet and our people from the consequences of climate change. Each of us can play a part in being a part of the solution by being more aware of our impact on others. This is the essence of creating a harmonious global and local community.

This book as its core is about global citizenship or the idea that all humans are a part of one global community on planet Earth. How we care for ourselves and our local communities directly impacts the global community.

COVID-19 was physical evidence of just how interconnected we are as a planet, as a human race. The first cases of this unknown virus was discovered in Wuhan, China in December 2019. By March 2020, COVID-19 was declared a global pandemic and subsequently much of the world went on quarantine or lockdown.

If one potentially deadly virus can spread from one country to the entire world in just three months, it shows how we are deeply interconnected and vulnerable to disease.

I dream it will become equally contagious to awaken to our power to heal ourselves and create a life of health, wealth and happiness. Would peace spread throughout the world like wildfire too? That is my dream. That is my hope for this book.

Being of Service to Humanity

If we can agree that all life is interconnected, the desire to serve others is important because our actions impact one another. My mother and her sister, my Auntie Grace, were always volunteering. They led regular community activities like prayer groups, and served food and raised money for the Veterans of Foreign War (VFW).

Being raised in a strong family that modeled community service, I always had a passion to help others. In high school, I also realized the environment was in trouble and I wanted to do something about it.

In college, I became active in the environmental justice movement. I worked and volunteered for numerous organizations that were working to resolve pollution in the US and in the Philippines. I marched in protests against the War in Iraq and was active in fighting for the human rights of gay people, women and people of color.

My last year at San Francisco State University, I received a Community Service Learning Award for my volunteer work with F.A.C.E.S.; Filipino American Coalition for Environmental Solutions, which was an organization that led campaigns to gain justice for Filipino communities in the Philippines negatively affected by pollution caused by the US military and corporations. I was able to travel to the Philippines with F.A.C.E.S. to witness firsthand the environmental injustices that Filipinos were facing.

Today, I am no longer on the front lines protesting but I do consider myself an *artivist*—I use my art to affect social change. I communicate a message of awakening to truth, love, freedom and justice through my poems, books, songs, plays and films. Art is a powerful unifying force that bridges differences between people and promotes harmony and peace.

Now, my passion lies in social entrepreneurialism: creating a business that promotes social good or solves a social problem. Within traditional capitalism, the business model puts profit over the health and well-being of people and the planet.

This has affected the state of our environment from deforestation, soil degradation and melting glaciers caused by pollution. It has also increased poverty and homelessness due to a lack of support for those with mental illness and lack of education.

Now more than ever do we need visionaries to use their talent to heal, protect and preserve our communities and our environment so it can continue to provide for us.

The dynamics of a healthy community require us to do our part by being accountable for our impact. It is our collective responsibility to see that we are contributing our resources and energy to solutions like education, self-empowerment, holistic health, job creation, and not be a part of society's problems.

We must go beyond the "normalized," unhealthy choices and lifestyles, and employ healthy ways of being that elevate our lives and the lives of those around us. If we can fuse the philosophy of global interconnectedness with our work, that is progress in the right direction.

A famous quote that first South African president Nelson Mandela used in his inaugural speech is by American writer and spiritual teacher, Marianne Williamson. It states "Our deepest fear is not that we are inadequate. Our deepest fear is that we are powerful beyond measure. It is our light, not our darkness that most frightens us..You are a child of God. Your playing small does not serve the world..We are all meant to shine, as children do. We were born to manifest the glory of God that is within us..It is not just in some of us; it is in everyone and as we let our own light shine, we unconsciously give others permission to do the same. As we are liberated from our own fear, our presence automatically liberates others."

Everyone has a mission or a unique gift we can use to create value for ourselves and others. When we cultivate our passions and skills, they lead us to our community, our tribe of people, who reflect our values and mission. Once we find a purpose that is aligned with our gifts, we inspire others to do the same and contribute to creating a legacy of peace for generations to come.

The Importance of Mentorship

The idea of mentorship is as ancient as family. Usually, our first mentors, teachers or guides are our parents, siblings and extended family. Even without verbal instructions, our families modeled behavior to us, for better or for worse.

When I became an adult, it was clear to me that beyond the education we receive from college professors, there was still much to learn. When it came to my career and in business, I was always aligned to someone ahead of me, who saw my potential and supported me to reach my next level whether this was in business, meditation or healing.

In some cases, you may need to do research to find the right mentor for whatever you want to do. I have had success in going to events that aligned with my passion to meet mentors and peers. With the Internet and the vast virtual community, limitless knowledge is available to us now. By researching the internet with a clear intention, everything is there to discover.

Today's mentors can be likened to career or life coaches. They mentor individuals or groups—in business, finance, marketing, media, healthy lifestyles, overcoming grief, overcoming addiction...you name it.

Giving back when we gain success recognizes that we are all connected. It acknowledges that my success is a result of the mentors, or many teachers that shaped me and contributed to the success that I am today.

One organization in the Bay area I produced a video for was called "Wardrobe for Opportunity," which provided job interviewing skills and business attire for low income people when interviewing and after they got the job. There are so many inventive ways to give back. We just need to honor the spirit of community and infuse this value into our life's work.

By giving back and through providing resources like environmental restoration, education, financial support, employment and more, we continue to honor the universal law of the interconnection of all people and help to preserve the abundance and well-being of our global community and planet to thrive for generations to come.

Chapter 8: Reflections:
In what ways can you build stronger community connections?

Chapter 9

Financial Literacy: Money is Energy, Access and Experience

Money is energy. It isn't good or bad. Depending on who has money and what they do with it, money can create a positive or negative effect.

Money is a tool we need to survive and thrive. You need money to eat, to have a place to live, to buy clothes, to get an education, to travel—to live. To look at money negatively is to misunderstand its necessity, power and usefulness.

I understand why there are negative perceptions about money. Some people with money or political power like politicians, military leaders and heads of corporations, abuse their power by exploiting workers and our environment.

But their actions are a reflection of their character and values but money itself is not to blame.

Money is freedom. I didn't see it that way until I had enough money to be free. Free to travel, free to stay in new places and eat whatever I want. I realized money is access to new experiences. Everyone should know how this freedom feels like.

But we are taught that financial freedom is something that is unattainable. The closest thing to it that we are modeled is called "retirement," reserved for employees that are 65 years or older, but who wants to wait that long?

Today with technology and the Internet, more younger people are becoming financially free as entrepreneurs earlier in life.

Success depends on hard work, good fortune and most importantly, an understanding of how to attract and sustain money. The latter is the most important because it's something that you have control over.

Developing a wealthy mindset is the starting point. There are many books on this topic. My favorite is "Secrets of the Millionaire Mind: Mastering the Inner Game of Wealth" by T. Harv Eker. He likens the mind to a hard drive with files; some are outdated and some are useful. He addresses the erroneous views we carry about wealth from our family or culture and uses declarations to help reprogram our "database" with new files that attract and generate wealth.

We all have different karma or fortune. Some are born into wealthy families, some are middle class, working class and some have nothing. Whatever the circumstance, we can learn how to transform and improve our situations. It requires self-awareness, motivation to learn, determination to improve, humility to receive guidance and persistent action that can change our finances.

By cultivating a mindset of wealth, developing a lucrative skill set and gaining an understanding of business, marketing and finance, you can create a thriving business to sustain your needs and create value for others.

The Capitalist Roots of Global Economics and Its Impact on Human and Environmental Health

Capitalism is the economic system of the United States and most of the world in which industry and trade are controlled by private owners for the accumulation of profit.

This system to maximize profit fits well with the desire of oppressive political forces to maintain control over people and the environment. The nature of capitalist values can be seen in every sector of society.

For instance, the profit-driven U.S. medical industry in the US that started in 1910 with the Flexner Report shifted focus from effective naturopathic medicines and modalities to an allopathic approach of "a pill for an ill," which within that system is now the only pathway to healing.

Just look at the statistics of how illness, death, the high cost of insurance, surgery and pharmaceutical dependency are putting people in debt. Capitalist values have prioritized profits over healing people of their illnesses.

Capitalism has impacted the education system. According to Best Colleges, in the last 15 years US student loan debt has tripled from $545 billion in 2007 to $1.75 trillion in 2022 (Ref. 196). Going into debt for a college education is normalized now more than ever. It's called "good debt" and still does not guarantee employment.

Needing a college degree to have a successful career is debatable. Some of the most successful billionaires in the world never went to college or dropped out. Some of them are Microsoft co-founder Bill Gates, Facebook CEO Mark Zuckerberg, Apple co-founder Steve Jobs, fashion designer Ralph Lauren and Grammy-award winning rapper/producers Jay Z and Sean "Puff Daddy" Combs to name a few.

One who was critical of the way we are educated in classrooms is Brazilian teacher and writer Paolo Friere who theorized that the mainstream approach to teaching, or pedagogy, is designed to keep people oppressed.

In his landmark 1968 work, "Pedagogy of the Oppressed," he likens "teachers as bank clerks depositing information into students rather than drawing out knowledge from individual students or creating inquisitive beings with a thirst for knowledge." (Ref. 130)

In the "banking" method everyone sits facing forward, as the teacher stands over and presents information like a banker. This model is used in Catholic churches, the religion in which I was raised. This power dynamic reinforces conformity through "following directions" and not questioning authority or having an opinion.

Friere asserts that the "banking" method of education mirrors the oppression in society by affirming these assumptions about the teacher (oppressor/owner) versus the student (people/workers): (Ref. 131)

- The teacher teaches and the students are taught
- The teacher knows everything and the students know nothing
- The teacher thinks and the students are thought about

- The teacher talks and the students listen – meekly
- The teacher disciplines and the students are disciplined
- The teacher chooses and enforces the choice, and the students comply
- The teacher chooses the program content, and the students (who were not consulted) adapt to it
- The teacher confuses the authority of knowledge with his or her own professional authority, which he or she sets in opposition to the freedom of the students
- The teacher is the subject of the learning process, while the pupils are mere objects

It's clear that most of us are indoctrinated in a way that steers us away from freedom and keeps us bound in a framework that does not value the experience of the individual nor the contribution of students.

This oppressive pedagogy reinforces the powerlessness of people within a political-socio-economic system that seeks to increase profits by exploiting people and the environment.

According to the Hunger Project, in 2021 there were 7.81 billion people in the world. Among those, 828 million people live in poverty and 99% of people live undernourished in mid to low-income countries. The accelerated rate of global hunger and poverty is a direct effect of "climate change, economic inequality and conflict" (Ref. 132).

The reverberating effects of capitalist values on the health and well-being of people and the environment are well-documented. This is especially true in developing countries and in underserved populations everywhere.

One solution is to shift from the capitalist value system to one that values human and environmental health. In 1994, a new model introduced by writer and entrepreneur John Elkington, known as the "Triple Bottom Line," seeks to gain profits while equally taking responsibility for the impact it has on people and the planet.

We need informed leaders and businesses to adopt these principles in their models to transform the way we define progress. If each person is aware of the global state of our world and given effective tools to create health, wealth and happiness, we can find solutions that don't feed into the problems we face as a planet.

Cuban revolutionary Fidel Castro said, "Capitalism has neither the capacity, nor the morality, nor the ethics to solve the problems of poverty…we must establish a new world order based on justice, on equity, and on peace" (Ref. 133).

Argentine revolutionary Che Guevara said "Above all, always be capable of deeply feeling any injustice committed against anyone, anywhere in the world…The true revolutionary is guided by a great feeling of love. It is impossible to think of a genuine revolutionary lacking this quality" (Ref. 134).

These revolutionaries invested their lives for social change to help those who need it most, the poor and working class. They remind us that we must stand against social injustice for all people, regardless of status and identity.

Pedagogy of Soka Education: Value Creation

In 2007, I found Nichiren Buddhism led by SGI-USA or Soka-Gakkai, which means value creation through peace, culture and education. This philosophy and practice completely revolutionized my life.

Being raised in the US as a Roman Catholic, I was indoctrinated by the "banking" method and taught to follow rules and not question authority. However, I always felt a strong connection to my intuition and the inner wisdom of my spirit and my body.

Growing up, I was opinionated and had difficulty accepting certain ideologies and practices that conflicted with my own experience. For example, being queer and coming to terms with the anti-gay, homophobic beliefs of Christianity were challenging and traumatizing.

Once in my 20s, I was at church while visiting my family. The pastor gave a homophobic sermon and I walked out. I later told my Dad that I could not attend church anymore because of how the hateful speech made me feel. My Dad understood and from then on, I was excused from attending church. I then sought a spiritual practice that supported and respected my whole identity and not just parts of me.

At the age of 27 (Saturn's Return), I found Nichiren Buddhism and the SGI or Soka-Gakkai International. In this religion/spiritual practice, I encountered a humanistic philosophy that honors the whole person, regardless of age, gender, sexuality or ethnicity. It was the first religion that I felt safe and empowered to fully be who I am.

The founders of Nichiren Buddhism SGI or Soka-Gakkai (value creation) International were teachers from Japan during World War II. They were critical of teaching students as if they were objects. They applied this value-creation pedagogy to teaching that honored the entire student with their own experience of learning and communicating.

They took the humanistic principles of Soka-Gakkai and created Soka education based on peace, human rights and the sanctity of life. In this framework, open and free dialogue is encouraged, and a deep appreciation for human diversity is at the forefront.

Today at Soka University in Southern California, founded by SGI president Daisaku Ikeda, their values state "Education is an integrating process in which students gain an awareness of the interdependence of themselves, others, and the environment. Wisdom, courage, and compassion—values treasured by the university—do not exist in isolation. They emerge in individuals as they learn the importance of service to others, to the natural world around them, and to the great cause of peace and freedom."

SGI meetings are also based on these principles. They are a safe space to fully express myself, teach from my own wisdom and feel seen, heard and accepted.

During smaller meetings, we sat in circle communication so everyone could see each other and participate on the same level. While serving as an SGI leader for 10 years, I came to understand that humanity could exist in a harmonious way, respectful of differences while honoring our own uniqueness.

President Daisaku Ikeda has sent annual World Peace Proposals to the United Nations for over 40 years on how applying Soka values can advance world peace by "recognizing the interconnection of all human life by encouraging nuclear disarmament, dialogue as an answer to war, increasing human security by ensuring equal education of all people, compassion for others and defending and celebrating the diversity of life" and more (Ref. 136).

What a different world we'd have if our social systems were based on Soka values. We can create a new world by developing businesses that infuse humanistic values like bringing back honor, healing the Earth and valuing each person's worth.

My hope is that more people think about our long-term impact on the world and not just the short term of maximizing profits. We can make money while giving back. Our future depends on those willing to shift the paradigm and return to holistic values. What will be your impact?

Employee – Self-Employed – Entrepreneur

The "banking" method produces employees. Employees or "workers" are the cogs in the machine of a business. In the framework of capitalism, the owners have exclusive rights on decision making and earning profits off of the labor of their workers. This dynamic creates the dehumanizing treatment of workers, a lack of equal rights and inhumane working conditions.

As much as I love Apple, they outsource the production of their products to cheaper labor forces outside of the U.S. like to China. Despite earning billions in profits, when they learned some of their Chinese factories had a high suicide rate among overworked workers in their supply chain, with many jumping from windows during their shifts, they did not seek to resolve the issue. Instead, they asked "management to put nets outside the windows to catch jumpers and send them back to the production line" (Ref. 135).

In top-down economics, employees have a fixed ceiling on how much they have to work, how much they are paid and how much time they have off. This feeds into the pedagogy of the oppressed.

As an entrepreneur, I advocate for people to seek career paths that offer more freedom and pay. However, it takes all career paths for businesses to thrive. In my experience as an employee, employees are happiest when they have a good pay and benefits, mentored and supported, involved, appreciated, valued and empowered.

There are many companies now who provide a good work-life balance. Some companies now allow hybrid and remote options where you can work part time in an office and part from home or fully from anywhere in the world.

After I graduated college I developed media skills like photography, video production and DJing where I learned how to become self-employed. Being independent is my nature, so to be able to attract my own clients and set my own pay rate gave me more freedom and power than if I worked for someone else.

As a solopreneur, I still found it challenging to sustain my needs being completely self-employed so I always kept a part-time job so being self-employed was a side hustle for a long time.

The benefits of being an employee versus being self-employed versus being an entrepreneur vary in terms of the freedom of time, money and travel.

As an employee, most hardly have any time outside of work, and little to no money to travel.

While being self-employed, you have the freedom to set your own pay rate so you can have an increase in money but by working only one job as a solopreneur with one stream of income, you may still not have money or the freedom to travel.

Being an entrepreneur offers the most freedom. As an entrepreneur, you can have multiple streams of income with a mix of active and passive income. Active income is money that you earn in exchange for your time. Passive income is money you earn by doing little to no work.

Traditionally, it was a sign of wealth to have a house, car and assets in one place as an employee, then retire at the age of 65. But with the advancement of internet commerce and technology, younger people are achieving "early retirement" or financial freedom.

As a digital nomad with an online business, I have freedom in my finances, time and location now. I don't have to wait until I am older with less energy to enjoy my life. More people are waking up to the possibility of living a life of adventure now in the fast lane, rather than waiting for permission in the slow lane.

Time is our most precious asset. And we are our most precious investment. If we invest the time to develop skills and carry out a vision we are passionate about, then we can create a life that is more fulfilling and become our own boss.

Small businesses (and the entrepreneurs who start them) are the backbone of the economy. According to a study in 2019 conducted by the US Small Business Association (SBA), small businesses with 500 employees or fewer make up 99.9% of all paid employees, account for 44% of all US economic activity and 72% of new job creation (Ref. 137).

There are also business formations known as cooperatives which are run by a group of worker-owners where power is shared. So instead of owners taking all the profit and workers doing all the work, the workers do equal work and own equal shares of the business.

Arizmendi is a bakery in the Bay area that is a successful cooperative. One of my friends is a worker-owner there. They all do an equal load of the work, they each have a say in what happens in the business and at the end of the year they share profits.

My top reasons for why I love being an entrepreneur are that I have a unique vision for my life, I am creative with multiple talents, I am ambitious, I hate being told what to do, I get bored easily and I cannot sit for long periods of time.

The life of an entrepreneur requires more effort to establish, but the reward is freedom. On the path of an entrepreneur, there is no ceiling to how much money you can make or the amount of time you can take off. You are the boss.

We need more visionaries to offer services and products that promote the betterment of our world. Small businesses and entrepreneurs are the backbone of the economy. If you have a vision for a business that could improve the quality of life for others while bringing you happiness and the freedom to enjoy your life, the time is ripe to create the lifestyle you desire.

Passive Income, Assets and The Freedom of Online Business Models

Japanese American entrepreneur Robert Kiyosaki, author of "Rich Dad, Poor Dad" makes his point that you can't get rich from a paycheck (employee), you get rich from owning assets that make passive income then scale up.

Most people have liabilities which is anything you owe money to.

Passive income is where you make little to no effort to make money. Passive income can be generated from assets like stocks, bonds, real estate, savings or retirement accounts and business income.

As an entrepreneur with an online business, you can hire out labor to other people, then collect profits as an owner. Or with the freedom of the internet, you can automate your business so you don't have to pay for a staff or a storefront.

The new definition of an asset in the 21st Century is anything that makes money in your sleep. With an automated online business, you can have complete freedom at your fingertips. As an entrepreneur with online skills and digital tools to support your career, financial freedom is more possible. Just research it. Someone has figured it out and wants to teach you how to do it too.

US tax laws cater to these types of income. Employees are taxed at about 30%. Whereas on average, the tax percentage on small businesses is about 20% and on investment income is about 4%.

Today, many online businesses allow people to be self-employed, with more time and freedom. In the world of influence, on Twitter, anyone can be a reporter. On Instagram or Youtube, you can monetize your audience through ads and subscriptions.

Many Youtube influencers have broken into the mainstream like Lily Singh and Issa Rae, who both have successful shows on TV and film because of their internet beginnings.

One of my favorite Youtube influencer/digital creators, a high-school dropout, now a millionaire—Casey Neistat. He started gaining visibility as an independent filmmaker with his brother, when they sold their film "The Neistat Brothers" to HBO for just under $2 million.

Shortly after, Neistat made Youtube videos promoting social change that grabbed the attention of *Time, New York Magazine* and built his audience. In March of 2015, he began creating daily vlogs of his life in New York City. His unique storytelling skills and narrative devices have influenced many, including me.

To date, Casey has created over a thousand Youtube vlogs, reached over 12 million followers and was named GQ "New Media Star" of the year. He is an inspiration and evidence of what is possible with persistent passion for storytelling, filmmaking and building an online business on Youtube.

Other online platforms that offer new economy job paths with more independence while earning active/passive money are Amazon with dropshipping, Airbnb with rental income, Uber by becoming your own taxi, Bitcoin by becoming your own bank, and more.

The world of life coaches or modern-day mentors is the way many digital nomads are thriving. Everyone needs a teacher. You can become an online coach to help people with anything from improving health, eating better, building confidence or teaching whatever wisdom or knowledge you have—that can improve the lives of others.

As a coach, you can earn passive income by building an online library of information, then charging a monthly fee for people to access the information online. Another option to build an application (or app) that creates passive income through subscriptions.

Utilizing online coaches and classes is the way I have built upon many skills that I use today from songwriting, marketing, investing and even writing this book.

In May of 2022, I joined Matt Rudnitsky's "The Punchy Book Accelerator." While unemployed at 22 with no experience, he wrote his first short punchy book, under 200 pages, that made over $14,000 in a few months. Today, he's a bestselling author of numerous books and a coach, teaching budding authors like me how to create their first book from start to finish.

Through his program, I got linked to my amazing editor, Laura, a copywriter for over 25 years who has made me a better writer. This book is published under Matt's imprint Platypus Publishing which is also a benefit of his program.

Perhaps you are in the online business industry or just realizing this pathway is available to you. Either way, I hope to inspire people to turn side hustles into successful small businesses that improve people's lives or help to solve a social challenge while they become financially free. The time is ripe to build an online career in this thriving, new economy.

Work Ethics Around the World

At my last full-time job, being tied to a desk for eight hours a day felt unnatural and just plain boring. Out of 52 weeks in a year, I had only three weeks of paid leave. Despite making good money and working with nice people, I knew my full potential was more than this path.

This "Work-Life Balance" or lack thereof is normal for most people. It was not until I began to live-work-travel as a digital nomad to Italy, did I realize countries like Italy, Spain and Sweden take a long break in the middle of the workday to eat, rest and spend time with loved ones.

In the U.S., "workplace-related stress affects up to 80% of workers and costs between $150 to $300 billion. Plus, with little to no paid time off, you're working yourself into an early grave: stress is linked to the sixth leading cause of death" (Ref. 138).

In early 1970s Japan, "karoshi" or death by overwork, emerged as many workers suddenly died from heart attacks, strokes or committed suicide due to work stress. A 2016 government survey says karoshi happens to employees working an average 65-80+ hours/week and that one in five Japanese workers are at risk of death (Ref. 139).

Given the epidemic of death from overwork, the US, Japan and other countries could learn from our European counterparts about the need to adopt values that balance life and work to improve health and prevent deaths that negatively impact families and the economy.

"Fika" in Sweden is a mandatory part of the workday where employees bond and relax over "fikabread," a pastry and coffee. It's proven to increase productivity and efficiency.

In Italy, "Riposo" is when business owners close between 12pm to 4pm to go home and enjoy an extended lunch break. In Spain, "Siesta" refers to an afternoon nap traditionally taken by farmers to avoid the hottest hours of the day. Siesta is preserved in much of Spain and is said to improve mood and performance. "Tea time" in Great Britain and "Merienda" in Argentina also include taking a break from work to improve the mental health and quality of life of employees.

One way to combat the lack of work-life balance is to become an entrepreneur. If you have a vision for a business or a passion that creates value for others, why not pursue it? It will take more work but the reward is freedom!

As an entrepreneurial digital nomad, I get up when I want, choose who I want to work with and where I want to work, decide how long I want to work and relax and play when I want. The freedom of being your own boss is priceless and one I would not trade for anything. It is not a path for everyone, but I believe more people are awakening to creating their own path of self-employment, financial freedom and happiness.

Chapter 9: Reflections:
In what ways can you create more financial freedom?
In what ways can you create more work-life balance?

Chapter 10

Sustainability: Honoring Our Global Interconnectedness

The Alarm Has Sounded

"When the last tree has been cut down, the last fish caught, the last river poisoned, only then will we realize that one cannot eat money." -Cree Indian prophecy.

Sustainability is a value system and set of practices that support the long-term environmental, economic and social health of the planet and its inhabitants. We have seen what the opposite of sustainability creates when short-term profits are prioritized and the well-being of the environment and people are excluded from the equation.

In modern society, we need money to survive. But it's clear that we've lost our way when it comes to living in harmony with the Earth.

When capitalist agendas and profit-driven social systems dictate the way we use energy, what materials we use, what medicines are available to us to "heal" us, and what foods are "safe" for us to eat, we are left with the status quo.

We must step outside of the "prescribed" way of living and question if the path we are on is one that is best for our health, our families, our communities and our planet. We must look at the impact of our actions.

The biggest contributor to climate change is the use of fossil fuels or non-renewable energy resources. Oil, coal and gas, which all contribute to the accumulation of carbon dioxide and greenhouse gas in our atmosphere.

These gasses get trapped, increase the temperature of our planet, and have a destructive impact on our environment. For one, global warming is accelerating the melting of our polar ice caps. The resulting increase of water contributes to more extreme weather events, like heavy rainfall, flooding and droughts.

It does not take a scientist to look around and see that there is something wrong with our environment. Destructive hurricanes are becoming more frequent as in 2005 when a rare category five, Hurricane Katrina, hit New Orleans with winds over 150 miles per hour and the surrounding areas. Katrina flooded over 80% of the city, killing over 1300 people and costing over $140 billion to recover (Ref. 140).

Environmental imbalance can be seen as entire coastal cities are being swept away from rising tides. In May 2023 in Emilia Romagna, Italy, six months' worth of rainfall fell in 36 hours displacing over 36,000 residents from their homes (Ref. 141).

FloodList, a think tank based in Germany, uses science and technology to keep global communities informed. In this changing climate, everyone is susceptible to the threat of flooding.

FloodList estimates that "Between 1995-2015, as many as 157,000 people died as a result of flooding. During that time, at least 2.3 billion people were affected by floods" (Ref. 142). FloodList claims that regular flooding is our new normal.

I've witnessed an uptick in flooding first-hand from living in coastal cities. From growing up in Washington, D.C. to my travels in Mexico, I have seen flash floods dump out a foot of water in just hours causing havoc. This is our wake-up call to take action.

The alarm sounded decades ago that fossil fuel energy is heating up the planet, creating imbalances in our ecology. But many more still need to understand how our actions contribute to environmental devastation and how to change our behavior to turn the tide.

Former U.S. Vice President Al Gore, a long time advocate of environmental activism began the "first congressional hearings on climate change, and co-sponsor[ed] hearings on toxic waste and global warming" at the age of 28 in 1976.

In 2006, Gore produced a documentary called "An Inconvenient Truth" to educate people on the destructive effects of fossil fuel use, climate change and the impact it will have on our cities. He revealed the acceleration of climate change due to human activity with flood simulations showing how our coastlines will change as we know them. After the film, I was hopeful that our U.S. energy system would move toward more sustainable energy sources.

But even after the film's release over 15 years ago, according to the Energy Information Administration, the U.S. runs on over 80% non-renewable or fossil-fuel energy and is the top producer of oil (Ref. 147). The U.S., China, India, Russia and Japan are the top polluters of the planet (Ref. 152).

CO2 emissions are the bulk of the damaging pollution that comes from the burning of oil for transportation and burning coal for electricity. This is what is called our "carbon footprint."

Because of rampant deforestation of our planet, the trees that once helped to absorb CO2 and release oxygen are disappearing.

According to Greenpeace, as much as 80% of the world's forests have been destroyed or irreparably degraded (Ref. 149).

The head of the International Energy Agency (IEA), Fatih Birol said that "the global oil and gas industry's profits on average grossed up $1.5 trillion in recent years, but in 2022 jumped to some $4 trillion (Ref. 150).

It's concerning that even after someone as prominent as Al Gore sounded the alarm, there have been no major changes made. It's business as usual when profits are still valued more than the well-being of the people and the planet. We must all learn what we can do to be a part of the solution.

Connecting the Dots: What is Climate Change?

When I was in high school in the mid-1990s, I had a passion for environmental education and activism. I had a poster on my bedroom wall called, "The State of the Atmosphere." It showed different layers of pollution from greenhouse gas, CFCs and so on, with clean air being the top layer of the atmosphere.

I knew our planet was in trouble and I wanted to be a part of saving our home. I'll never forget 1995, when a huge section of the Antarctic glaciers known as Larsen A, about 25 times the size of Manhattan, broke off of the ice shelf and drifted into the ocean (Ref. 143).

Scientists still have trouble estimating how long the ice shelves will take to melt and how much they will cause our tides to rise. But as you can see, global flooding has been the immediate result for decades and continues to threaten human and planetary health.

Glaciers have melted throughout time, however melting increased around the 1900s after the rise of the Industrial Revolution.

The Industrial Revolution increased the development of urban areas, which accelerated the release of carbon dioxide and greenhouse gas from vehicles and factories into our atmosphere. This causes temperatures to rise and speeds up the melting of polar caps.

Then there is the rampant deforestation of our planet, most especially the destruction of the Amazon, the largest rainforest in the world. The Amazon and all forests are like the lungs of the Earth; they help absorb carbon dioxide and produce fresh oxygen for us to breathe.

Large rainforests and forests help keep the Earth cool so with the loss of trees, greenhouse gas and rising sea levels, have dramatically increased over the last few decades.

The Importance of Biodiversity to Human and Environmental Health

The Amazon rainforest also is one of the most biodiverse places on the Earth, housing over 3 million species, including over 2,500 tree species (Ref. 144). Biodiversity supports many environmental functions that the entire ecology, including humans, rely on to survive.

Environmental organization Client Earth works in over 50 countries, with people, campaigners, governments and industry to create solutions to the most pressing environmental challenges.

Client Earth defines biodiversity as "the natural world around us, the variety of all the different kinds of organisms—the plants, animals, insects and microorganisms that live on our planet. Every one of these live and work together in ecosystems to maintain and support life on Earth, and exist in delicate balance" (Ref. 145).

Greenpeace, a non-profit dedicated to protecting the environment from destruction, explains that biodiversity supports processes that "purify water, make air breathable, control outbreaks of diseases and pests, support pollination, build fertile soils, and store carbon. [It is] makes a place breathe, live, and stay healthy and beautiful" (Ref. 144).

According to the National Institute of Health, the loss of biodiversity due to climate change increases the risk of zoonotic diseases, which means pathogens from non-human animals can pass more easily to humans now.

COVID-19 is an example of how serious the risk is now. The disease originated in bats from Wuhan, China. The disease then spread to the Huanan Seafood Wholesale Market in Wuhan which was the source of all cases, infecting people who ate food from there in December of 2019. The market was shut down by January 2020 (Ref. 146).

By March 11, 2020, COVID-19 was documented to have infected "more than 118,000 cases in 114 countries and 4,291 deaths. Only three months after its discovery, the WHO (World Health Organization) declares COVID-19 a pandemic (Ref. 146).

According to the *Intergovernmental Science-Policy Platform on Biodiversity and Ecosystem Services,* "almost 1 million species are currently facing extinction. This rate has largely picked up in the last 40 years, with threatened and vulnerable species across taxa" (Ref. 144).

Those most affected by climate change are poor people because they do not have the means to protect themselves or relocate in the event of a natural disaster. Also under the greatest risk of environmental threat are indigenous people and the lands they inhabit. Indigenous people are keepers of ancient wisdom of how to live in harmony with the land and its inhabitants. They hold the keys to knowledge on how to use the Earth's natural resources to sustain life and heal ourselves.

Because of their spirituality, sense of community, livelihood and lifestyles are based on the health of the Earth, indigenous people lives are "threatened by environmental degradation, large scale industrial activities, toxic waste, conflicts and forced migration, as well as by land-use and land-cover changes (such as deforestation for agriculture and extractives of precious materials). These challenges are further exacerbated by climate change" (Ref. 152).

In the Philippines, climate change has "increased flooding, landslides and tropical cyclones—forcing entire communities from their homes" (Ref. 153). The Inuit people in Alaska, Canada and Greenland and indigenous people everywhere face similar issues of "flooding, loss of land, displacement, political and economic marginalization, human rights violation, discrimination and unemployment" (Ref. 154).

The irony is that those most negatively impacted by climate change contribute the least to the greenhouse gas emissions that cause it.

What Solutions Can We Employ?

Conscious consumerism is the idea that we can affect positive social change by being intentional with where we spend our money. We can choose to support businesses that promote sustainable values and take into consideration the health of the environment and people.

You can research a company's ethics and practices that prioritize social responsibility over profits before buying from them. Buying "Fair Trade" certified goods ensure workers receive fair wages, improve living conditions and help to alleviate poverty.

Boycotting or divesting money from companies that do not value the health of people, animals or the environment is another way we can affect change.

The most successful boycott in the U.S. was the Montgomery Bus Boycott, led by Dr. Martin Luther King, Jr. and Rosa Parks, which lasted for almost 13 months starting December 5th, 1955. During the civil rights movement, King led his organization, the Montgomery Improvement Association (MIA), demanding equal rights for Black people to be able to sit anywhere on public buses and not be relegated and segregated to sit in the back because of their race.

At the start of the boycott, it was reported that almost 90% of Black citizens stayed off the bus (Ref. 156). But when demands were not met, the boycott was extended. Met with opposition, protesters served jail time and were mistreated, and even King's home was bombed.

After a long, hard-fought boycott, the Supreme Court ruled segregated seating on public buses were unconstitutional and no longer allowed.

In 1965, on Mexican Independence Day in Delano, California, Cesar Chavez and other Latino farm workers protested for humane working conditions and better wages for Filipino-American grape workers. The Delano Grape Strike lasted until 1970, which caused an international boycott, ultimately leading to the creation of the United Farm Workers of America, the United States' first farm workers union.

Reduce, Reuse, Recycle in the Face of the Global Landfill Crisis

The U.S. produces 268 million tons of trash annually which is high compared to other countries (Ref. 157). Most of the trash that ends up in a landfill is food or material that can be recycled like paper and plastic. The environmental issue with landfills is that they produce foul-smelling gas like ammonia and greenhouse gasses like methane and carbon dioxide that contribute to the climate crisis.

I remember taking road trips as a kid from D.C. to New York City and smelling the nasty odor of the Fresh Kills landfill in Staten Island when we would cross the New York state line. The Fresh Kills landfill spanned over 2,200 acres, being the world's largest landfill until its closure in 2001.

I also experienced Smokey Mountain, one of the largest landfills in one of the poorest parts of Manila, Philippines. It is dubbed Smokey Mountain because of the plumes of smoke from burning garbage and sits about 50 meters high. The most alarming part of my visit, besides the incomprehensible smell, is that the site was home to over 25,000 people. There were actual funerals being held on the trash heap. I can't imagine what the life expectancy is of someone who is born and raised in a toxic trash dump. The landfill was closed in 1995 and public housing was built in its place.

So what can we do to reduce our waste? We can consume less and reduce the waste we create by recycling paper, plastic, glass, aluminum and composting our food waste. We can also reuse containers or bring them when we get take-out at restaurants. We can invest in reusable grocery bags, coffee/tea-cups, water bottles, bamboo utensils or anything we use often to replace plastic. We can choose to purchase from companies that only use recycled material.

We can opt for paperless billing, use electronic documents to cut back on paper use and buy brands that used recycled paper. We can make efforts to buy used or secondhand items that can cut back on waste. Not only is this good for the environment, but for our pockets as well.

Parents can opt to use cloth diapers as opposed to disposable diapers that create methane, a greenhouse gas. Females can use medical grade silicone (or BPA-free which is nontoxic) menstrual cups for that time of the month, instead of contributing to environmental pollution. Menstrual cups are also better for your body. No TSS, toxic shock syndrome from tampons and no squishy sound or funny smell from pads. Just set it and forget it. Imagine how much money you can save too.

Over 10 years ago, I started using a Ruby Cup from a female-led, socially-responsible company that gives a cup to impoverished females in East Africa and other countries, when you buy one. They have donated over 142,000 cups in 15 countries since 2012. They also teach workshops and offer mentorship in these communities on menstrual care and reproductive health.

DivaCup is another female-led business started by a woman and her mother, concerned about preserving the safety of women's bodies and the health of the environment. DivaCup is B Corp Certified, which means it meets high standards of accountability, transparency on employee benefits and charitable giving.

Global Plastic Waste, Zero Plastics Policy and Renewable Alternatives

Plastic is in so many products we use, because of its durability, flexibility and resistance to corrosion. Plastic is made from a chemical process derived from petroleum or oil, which is a fossil fuel.

Plastic is problematic for several issues. It takes 500 - 1,000 years to decompose, about 1 million marine animals die every year due to plastic pollution and only 9% is recycled according to the Sustainable Ocean Alliance (Ref. 158). Lying between Hawaii and California, The Great Pacific Garbage Patch is the world's biggest ocean waste heap, covering two times the size of Texas, with 1.8 billion pieces of floating plastic, estimated to kill thousands of marine animals every year (Ref. 159).

The United Nations estimates that every minute one garbage truck of plastic is dumped into our ocean (Ref. 157). In the last 60 years, over 7-9 billion tons of plastic has been produced and ended up in landfills or our planet's waters (Ref. 157).

Plastic has also entered our food chain. When fish and other animals consume plastic that they mistake for food and we eat them, then we are also consuming plastic. Plastic contains harmful chemicals that cause cancer, infertility, heart disease, stroke and other issues that pose serious health risks for all species.

Globally, we have come to the point where recycling while still needed and helpful is not enough. In response, some nations are adopting a "zero plastics" or "plastic free" policy to mitigate the issue. Countries like Canada, Portugal and Japan are beginning to ban "single use plastics" which are plastic products used only once then disposed of, like shopping bags, utensils, containers and straws. Instead they offer sustainable materials that biodegrade and do not pose a health risk.

Sustainable businesses are answering the call by refusing plastic products using renewable materials instead like bamboo, coconut, glass, cornstarch and wood. When I dined at a restaurant in Costa Rica, instead of disposable straws they had reusable stainless steel straws. Costa Rica is leading the way in employing sustainable materials, practices and energy all over the country.

From a planetary health perspective, refusing single-use plastics while using our own reusable item will cut down our waste impact.

We can invest in reusable straws made of bamboo or stainless steel, bring our own containers when we order take-out, buy a reusable water bottle and more. Glass or copper water bottles are the safest option and have no taste. Documented in ancient Egypt and Ayurvedic texts, copper vessels were used to store water for long periods as a way to kill bacteria (Ref. 171). Known as the "Oligodynamic effect," copper metal ions kill and inhibit the growth of microorganisms. Using copper for food and drink items has many health benefits like fighting off cancer, balancing hypertension, preventing inflammation, aiding digestion, anti-aging properties and more (Ref. 172).

With more awareness and intention with each choice we make, we can begin to transform the harmful ways we have negatively impacted the Earth, while reducing harm to ourselves.

Being Selective About What We Eat and Where Our Food Comes From

Monoculture or monocropping farming is when one crop is grown at a time on a specific area of land. This practice does not support biodiversity, increasing the risk of disease and pests. This type of farming is common especially for soybeans, wheat and corn, which are often genetically modified. Monoculture uses chemical fertilizers, depletes soil, pollutes waterways and encourages more methane emissions, all of which are bad for the environment.

Permaculture is the ethical principle of creating a closed sustainable ecosystem that cares for the Earth, the people and the community and creates no waste.

Permaculture was conceived in the 1970s by two Australians, Bill Mollinson and David Holmgren. They were interested in developing "permanent agriculture" or "permaculture." In 1978, their book "Permaculture One–A Perennial Agriculture for Human Settlements" takes "ideas from many areas—farming systems, traditional agriculture, building design and construction, water supply, ecology, anthropology, ethnobotany, technology and more—and synthesized them into something seemingly complete and achievable" (Ref. 155).

However, the roots of permaculture originated from indigenous cultures focused on how to grow food and support livestock based on sustainable systems that support regrowth. This value system stems from a spiritual belief that we, humans are too, a part of the Earth so it is our responsibility to revere and protect all of nature.

Growing our own food and supporting local, organic farms is one way to combat climate change as well as eat better for our health. Community gardens are popping up around the world as a means for communities to have fresh fruits and vegetables to eat and increase food security. A community garden is a place to gather through gardening which improves physical and mental health, improves air and soil quality, increases biodiversity and provides a place to compost, reducing food waste (Ref. 173).

The animal agriculture industry has a major impact on climate change. Unsustainable cattle ranches account for about 70% of the deforestation of the Amazon (Ref. 170). Factory produced meats and farmed seafood are not only bad for the environment but your health too. Farmed seafood and factory produced animals are fed harmful chemicals as opposed to wild seafood or organic meats where animals eat from the natural environment and ingredients which are better for you.

The act of going vegan or vegetarian is a way of boycotting the meat industry and its destructive ways on the environment. But if that's not your choice or physically possible for you, buying organic meats and wild seafood from sustainable businesses is another way to support those who are being ethically responsible about their long term impact on human and environmental health.

The Slow Movement

The term "slow movement" was popularized by Carlo Petrini when he protested the opening of McDonald's in Piazza di Spagna, Rome in 1986. Being critical of the notion that faster is better, he wanted to bring back the value of quality over quantity and bring mindfulness to our lives (Ref. 169). Slow living as a solution to the chaotic fast-paced lifestyle based on capitalism and consumerism and to be more present by taking our time to enjoy and savor each moment. This quality of slowing down has influenced many facets of our culture like work, food, parenting and fashion.

The Slow Food organization that began in Italy now spans over 150 countries, educating people on the health risk of fast food, genetically modified organisms (GMOs) and pesticides, promoting organically grown food, family farms and regional foods and traditions, and teaching gardening and ethical buying (Ref. 169).

"Slow food" as opposed to fast food, encourages consumers to support local businesses and local produce, often organically grown, to protest overproduction and food waste. Taking the time to cook my own meals is a type of therapy that is relaxing and eating slowly is better for your digestion. It also encourages creativity, good food, nutrition and the gathering of families and communities around home cooking or dining at local restaurants that support local farmers.

Chef and food activist, Alice Waters' book "We Are What We Eat: A Slow Food Manifesto," discusses her journey of promoting slow food when she opened her renowned restaurant "Chez Panisse" in Berkeley, California in 1971. Waters kick-started the "farm-to-table" movement dating back to the 1960's hippie movement in response to processed foods and produce being picked before ripening (which loses its taste) just to travel from country to country increasing our carbon footprint. Farm-to-table is about making tasty, handmade dishes from locally sourced, organic ingredients as a way to support nutrition, biodiversity and enjoy the hospitality of small, intimate dining for our communities.

"Slow Fashion" or sustainable fashion coined by Kate Fletcher in 2007, is also opposed to mass produced clothing or "fast fashion" and promotes local, handmade clothing to reduce waste and overconsumption. Some slow fashion practices are boycotting producers of "fast fashion," buying secondhand or smaller, local businesses that are fair trade, or made from sustainable or recycled materials, encouraging people to make their own clothing and just buy fewer clothes in general (Ref. 169).

Since 2012, the Slow Factory, an environmental and social justice nonprofit organization, has aimed to capture the "intersections of climate and culture to build partnerships and communities to advance climate-positive global movements through the lens of human rights, science, technology, and fashion." Their work has been supported by Adidas, Google, Tesla and featured on Forbes, CNN, Scientific American and more.

Ending Our Fossil Fuel Addiction and the Need for Renewable Energy

When I visited Costa Rica in 2022, I went paddle boarding on beautiful Lake Arenal. My tour guide shared that Costa Rica runs on over 98% renewable energy and that over half of the country's energy alone is generated at the bottom of the lake through hydroelectric turbines, a technology developed in the 1800s.

Renewable energy aka "clean energy" is electricity generated from the sun, wind, water, waste, and heat from the Earth that does not harm human and environmental health and is replenishable. Fossil fuels aka "dirty energy" like oil, coal and gas are finite resources that require destructive practices to extract and still account for "over 80% of the world's energy"(Ref. 161).

In 1997, The Kyoto Protocol to the United Nations Framework Convention on Climate Change, was an international agreement aimed to reduce carbon dioxide (CO_2) emissions and greenhouse gas produced by industrialized nations to lessen their CO_2 emissions. In 2015, world leaders at the UN Climate Change Conference (COP21) created "The Paris Agreement" to reduce carbon emissions to limit the planet's rising temperature by 1.5 degrees which scientists call the "tipping point," where damage to our ecosystem will be irreversible (Ref. 162). Today, both agreements are backed by over 192 countries yet these political documents are still not enough to stop our climate issues.

Scientists theorize that we have already reached the tipping point at just 1.1-1.2 degrees rise in temperature seen in "loss of sea ice in the Arctic adding to regional warming, accelerating ice melt from Greenland, and massive bushfires in Australia and the third mass bleaching of the Great Barrier Reef in only five years" (Ref. 164).

Renewable energy is not only healthier and safer, it's also cheaper and creates new jobs. According to the UN, "net-zero emissions (only clean energy) will lead to an overall increase in energy sector jobs: while about 5 million jobs in fossil fuel production could be lost by 2030, an estimated 14 million new jobs would be created in clean energy, resulting in a net gain of 9 million jobs" (Ref. 163).

As global citizens, education and action is needed now more than ever. We need to elect world leaders who have the values and wisdom to change to renewable energy for the best interest of humans and environmental health.

Transportation is the largest source of greenhouse gas emissions in the U.S. Ways we can reduce our carbon footprint include using bikes, electric bikes, walking, carpooling, public transport and electric/hybrid vehicles. Not only are these options better for the environment but also better for your pockets and your health.

Sustainable public transit such as electric buses, streetcars, trolleys, and high-speed trains that run on renewable energy is also a step in the right direction. In the San Francisco Bay Area, BART, or Bay Area Rapid Transit, the public train system, is committed to running on 50% renewable energy by 2025 (Ref. 168). Hydrogen fuel cell-powered buses, which do not emit CO_2, can be found on the road in California too (Ref. 168).

Electric cars, which run solely on battery and hybrid cars, which run on batteries and gas, have come a long way. While the price tag can still run high as in the case with Tesla, more models like the Chevy Bolt and Nissan Leaf, offer more affordable options.

The last car I owned was the Toyota Corolla Hybrid which starts at $23,000 USD which is the cheapest one on the market. I could drive that car for four hours from DC to New York City and still have a half tank of gas left which was a big money saver. Over 10 million electric cars were sold worldwide in 2022 and is expected to increase by 35% in 2022 (Ref. 166).

Electric cars have lithium batteries which are toxic to the environment but there are ways they can be disposed of safely. It is estimated if the US "transitions to 100% electric cars sales by 2035 and 100% electric trucks by 2040, as well as using 100% renewable energy sources such as solar, wind, hydroelectric and nuclear by 2035," then there would be a "92% fall in greenhouse gas by 2050, generating $1.7 trillion for the environment, resulting in 110,000 fewer deaths, 2.8 million fewer asthma attacks and avoid 13.4 million sick days by 2050" (Ref. 167).

Solar energy companies are on the rise and today there are solar energy leasing programs for homeowners to invest in solar panels at 0% down to generate renewable energy for their home and start saving immediately. My uncle works with a company called Pulsar that offers free solar panel installation to homeowners in Maryland and Virginia. My mother took advantage of this and saved money on her energy bill.

Not only is solar energy good for the planet but it's also a big money saver. Any excess energy generated goes back to feed to the energy grid called "net metering" which can offset homeowners' energy costs or result in a rebate.

Several countries lead the way in running on mostly renewable energy with the goal of "net zero" which means when the amount of carbon emitted is equal to the amount of carbon being removed from the atmosphere.

Costa Rica has been running on over 98% renewable energy using hydro, wind, solar and more renewable sources for over seven years now and has generated more energy than needed so they have exported it to other countries (Ref. 165). Uruguay also generates 98% of its electricity on renewable energy like wind and solar, exporting its excess energy to neighboring countries, Brazil and Argentina (Ref. 165).

In 2011, Scotland generated just 37% renewable energy but by 2020, produced over 97% renewable energy for their electricity needs. Iceland runs almost 100% of its electricity on renewable energy, with 9 out of 10 homes running on geothermal power. In 2023, Norway generated 99% of its electricity from renewable energy, based mostly on hydropower since the late 1800s (Ref. 165).

We still need the countries with the largest carbon footprint like the U.S., China and India, to begin running on mostly renewable energy toward reaching net zero. These smaller countries serve as a model of those answering the call and adapting to help resolve the climate crisis we face as a planet.

Paying It Forward: Those Who Are Working To Protect The Planet

When most governments and corporations are still colluding to maintain our fossil fuel addiction by putting profit accumulation over people and planet, how do concerned global citizens step in to help resolve climate change? While there are too many to note, I will highlight some notable activists who lead the way in environmental and climate justice.

American biologist and author Rachel Carson is regarded as the "founder of the modern environmental movement" with her groundbreaking work, "Silent Spring" released in 1962. The controversial book outlined the environmental dangers of using pesticides like DDT as "biocides" that kill all forms of life. Her work would help ban DDT later.

Native American land rights activist and author Winona LaDuke founded the White Earth Land Recovery Project, focused on land recovery and preservation of spiritual and cultural traditions of her ancestors. In 1985, she established the Indigenous Women's Network, dedicated to increasing the visibility of Native women and empowering their participation in political arenas.

Twice nominated for the Nobel Peace Prize, David Brower was the first executive director of the Sierra Club, growing its membership tenfold. He also founded Friends of the Earth, a worldwide environmental network active in 52 countries, co-founded the League of Conservation Voter and founded the Earth Island Institute. The David Brower Center in his hometown of Berkeley, California, houses dozens of environmental organizations and holds art exhibits, educational programs and conferences that support community engagement and environmental justice.

Kenyan activist and professor, Wangari Maathai, started the Green Belt Movement in 1977, a tree planting initiative aimed at restoring our forests. The movement inspired individuals from other African nations to follow suit. The organization is estimated to have planted over 51 million trees to date. Maathai was awarded the Nobel Peace Prize in 2004 for her progress in advancing environmental restoration and conservation.

Swedish youth activist Greta Thunberg rose to fame when she gave an impassioned speech at the 2019 UN Climate Action Summit called, "How Dare You?" She aimed her words at world leaders' inaction toward resolving climate change, saying: "How dare you!

You have stolen my dreams and my childhood with your empty words. And yet I'm one of the lucky ones. People are suffering. People are dying. Entire ecosystems are collapsing. We are in the beginning of a mass extinction. And all you can talk about is money and fairytales of eternal economic growth. How dare you!" (Ref. 174)

Thunberg's recent work, "The Climate Book," is a compilation of writings she wants concerned citizens to read to mobilize for a sustainable future. It included short pieces by 100 authors, including scientists, biologists, journalists and economists, and Thunberg weaves the entire piece together.

The book is divided into five parts: "How Climate Works," "How Our Planet Is Changing," "How It Affects Us," "What We've Done About It," and "What We Must Do Now." Thurnberg's passion and leadership proves that the voices of youth must be heard. She says to her readers, "You must take it from here and carry on connecting the dots yourself because, right there, between the lines, you will find the answer—the solutions that need to be shared with the rest of humanity. And when the time comes for you to share them, I would give you just one piece of advice. Simply tell it like it is" (Ref. 175).

Many celebrities are active in fighting for climate change action including Jane Fonda, Meryl Streep and Mark Ruffalo. In 1998, Leonardo DiCarprio started a foundation in his name to sound the alarm on environmental issues, help protect endangered species and restore vulnerable ecosystems. His documentary on climate change, "The 11th Hour" raised $40 million, becoming the highest grossing environmental charity event.

Countless youth environmental activists are emerging from Iran, Samoa, Uganda, the Philippines and many other areas of the world most affected by climate change to do their part to educate and mobilize people to take action and rally government leaders to do more to resolve the climate crisis.

Founded in 1996 in Oakland, California, Amazon Watch is a nonprofit that works with indigenous people and environmental organizations to protect the Amazon rainforest and the human rights of indigenous communities in the Amazon basin in Peru, Columbia, Brazil and Ecuador. The Amazon is home to 400 indigenous peoples and the largest rainforest, producing up 20% of the world's oxygen. They work to resist deforestation by supporting Indigenous-led solutions to resolve climate change.

There are a number of Indigenous-led organizations working toward resolving the climate crisis like Futuros Indígenas or Indigenous Futures Network, which organizes and prioritizes indigenous narratives and human rights, Re:wild, a collaboration of conservation scientists and organizations working to protect the most biodiverse places on the planet and Global Witness, which holds companies and governments accountable for their environmental destruction.

Now more than ever, we need to address and protect the rights of indigenous people who protect and preserve almost 80% of the remaining biodiverse lands of the planet and who are on the frontlines of extinction (Ref. 181). By protecting those who give back to the planet, we can help to ensure the health of our planet and our future generations.

Answering The Call

In response to climate change, the best starting point is getting environmental education and becoming a part of the solution.

This book is a call to action: It's time to activate solutions that positively impact our own health and community wellness, which ultimately impacts our environment.

In addition to growing food to help offset environmental issues, people around the world are starting ecovillages or small, self-sufficient communities that live in harmony with nature. The idea is to build a community based on cooperation, using renewable energy and materials.

This model takes from ancient civilizations like the Mayans. They created sustainable communities called "solars," or places of social connection for families and friends within each unit to have their own garden for food, herbs and medicinal plants with compost and water filtration systems (Ref. 176).

I witnessed sustainable communities on Big Island of Hawaii. I stayed in large communities and in homes of people who lived off the grid, meaning they were not dependent on utility companies for their basic needs. One family I stayed with grew their own food and had solar panels for their electricity, a rainwater catcher and a filtration system for water.

The Global Ecovillage Network tracks sustainable communities around the world so people can find them to be a part of the movement. It is estimated there are over 10,000 ecovillages worldwide.

Some of the most inspiring communities living sustainably are those with the most residents who live to be over one hundred years old, or centenarians. These areas are called Blue Zones founded by Dan Buettner, a National Geographic Fellow.

He says that there are five Blue Zones on the planet: Okinawa, Japan, Sardinia, Italy, Ikaria, Greece, Loma Linda, California and Nicoya Peninsula, Costa Rica. All five areas share what is known as the "Power 9," key factors that sustain longer lives for those that live there.

The Power 9 Factors of Blue Zones (Ref. 177):

- Move naturally throughout day
- Have and cultivate a strong sense of purpose
- Downshift time everyday to relieve stress
- Eat until 80% full
- Mostly plant-based diet
- Having wine/food at end of day with friends
- Having a tribe, or strong community support
- Having loved ones and close friends
- Belonging to a faith-based or spiritual community

While traveling and writing this book, I synchronistically discovered the Blue Zones in Costa Rica and Sardinia, where the cost of living was low and the quality of life was high. I am fascinated by Blue Zones and have found that when I have these nine factors in place in my life, I am my healthiest and happiest.

I want to give love to the San Francisco Bay area in California where I lived for most of my adult life, and where I enjoyed having the "power 9." In this community, I learned much of what I am sharing with you in this book.

It's one of the most sustainable communities on the planet, where almost 81% of the people recycle with the goal of reaching zero waste (Ref. 178). It is home to many social justice movements and a place where I felt connected to a community that reflected my values for environmental and social justice as well as cultural diversity.

For this reason, people call it the "bubble." My hope is that this bubble can inspire, meet and unite with other bubbles or communities of conscious compassionate action toward creating a healthier, more just and sustainable world, where we can all live to be a hundred years old.

Chapter 10: Reflections:
How can you incorporate more sustainable practices in support of environmental wellness?

Reflection Questions for Book:

- Intro question: What is your self-care routine? What would you like to do better? (not listed in beginning)
- Ch. 1: What wellness activities do you do to maintain your mental health? How can you improve?
- Ch. 2: What ways can you integrate more natural foods and hydration to your current diet to feel and live better?
- Ch. 3: What ways can cannabis enhance your wellness?
- Ch. 4: How can entheogens help you heal your emotional trauma?
- Ch. 5: How can you support more inclusion of gender and sexuality diversity in your community?
- Ch. 6: How can you incorporate more daily self-loving activities?
- Ch. 7: What conflict resolution tools can you use to improve your relationships?
- Ch. 8: In what ways can you build stronger community connections?

- Ch. 9: In what ways can you create more financial freedom? In what ways can you create more work-life balance?
- Ch. 10: How can you incorporate more sustainable practices in support of environmental wellness?

Thank you for reading. Please share with loved ones. Please leave a review on Amazon if you feel moved to do so. To our health, wealth and happiness!! With love, Cynthia

References (from the internet):

Ref 1: Peter C Gøtzsche (2014) Our prescription drugs kill us in large numbers, *National Library of Medicine*
Ref 2: Lloyd Minor (2019) Why Medical Schools Need to Focus More on Nutrition, *Stanford School of Medicine*
Ref 3: American Society of Anesthesiologists (n.d.) Anesthesia Risks
Ref 4: Janet Martin (2019) More people die after surgery worldwide than from HIV, TB, and malaria combined
Ref 5: SGI Quarterly (1998) Who is a Buddha?
Ref 6: World Tribune (n.d.) The Mutual Possession of the Ten Worlds
Ref 7: World Health Organization (2022) COVID-19 pandemic triggers 25% increase in prevalence of anxiety and depression worldwide
Ref 8: United Nations (2022) What Is Climate Change?
Ref 9: Zach Stromberg (2013) Hippocrates: overcoming the fall
Ref 10: George F. Indest (2012) Doctors Under Pressure to Meet Quotas and Fill Hospital Beds
Ref 11: Shannon Brownlee & Judith Garber (2019) Overprescribed: High cost isn't America's only drug problem
Ref 12: Lown Institute (n.d.) Medication overload and older Americans
Ref 13: Leona Rajaee (2022) How many patients are most primary care physicians seeing?
Ref 14: Remy Franklin (2019) Are doctors spending less time with patients?
Ref 15: Andrea Boldt (2019) What Are the Benefits of Alkaline in the Body?
Ref 16: WebMD Editorial Contributors (2021) White Rice Linked to Diabetes Risk

Ref 17: INTERNATIONAL NETWORK OF CITIES WHERE LIVING IS GOOD (2014) DRAMATIC CORRELATION SHOWN BETWEEN GMOS AND 22 DISEASES
Ref 18: Nancy Swanson (2013) GMOs and Multiple Chronic Diseases
Ref 19: Hannah Nichols (2016) Wheat proteins may cause inflammation beyond the gut: Medical News Today
Ref 20: Dr. Ryan Bland (2020) Nightshades And Solanine Toxicity Syndrome
Ref 21: Joe Cross (n.d.) Reboot Success Stories
Ref 22: Parkview Health (2022) The importance of gut health
Ref 23: Prableen Bajpai (2022) What Countries Are the Top Producers of Oil?: Nasdaq
Ref 24: Climate Trade (2021) Which countries are the world's biggest carbon polluters?:
Ref 25: Rochester Institute of Technology (RIT) (n.d.) Global Interconnectedness
Ref 26: Quote Investigator® (2011) When the Last Tree Is Cut Down, the Last Fish Eaten, and the Last Stream Poisoned, You Will Realize That You Cannot Eat Money
Ref 27: Abrahm Lustgarten (2020) How Climate Change Is Contributing to Skyrocketing Rates of Infectious Disease
Ref 28: Elevation Now Wellness Center (2021) How Rockefeller Founded Big Pharma and Waged War on Natural Cures: multiple sources
Ref 29: Nila Eslit (2019) Health Benefits of Intermittent Fasting
Ref 30: Rachael Ajmera, MS, RD (2023) 8 Health Benefits of Fasting, Backed by Science: Healthline
Ref 31: By Sara Lindberg (2023) Autophagy: What You Need to Know: Healthline
Ref 32: LEO GIOSUÈ (2019) CBD is Here to Stay: 10 Mind-Blowing Health Benefits of CBD Oil: The Jerusalem Post
Ref. 33: Adda Bjarnadottir, MS, RDN (2023) 6 Evidence-Based Health Benefits of Hemp Seeds: Healthline
Ref. 34: VISHAL VIVEK (2019) The Usages Of Every Part Of Hemp Plant: Hemp Foundation
Ref 35: MaryAnn De Pietro, CRT (2021) What to know about endocannabinoids and the endocannabinoid system
Ref 36: Daniel Clark, The King's University (2021) The Impact of the Flexner Report on Sectarian Medical Schools
Ref 37: Eric Schmidt (2019) How Rockefeller Created the Business of Western Medicine

Ref. 38: Cannabinoid (n.d.) Wikipedia
Ref. 39: Crystal Raypole (2020) Cannabis Got You Paranoid? How to Deal With It
Ref. 40: Dario Sabaghi (2021) A Brief History Of The False Myth About Cannabis As A Gateway Drug, Forbes
Ref. 41: Matt Thompson (2013) The Mysterious History Of 'Marijuana," NPR
Ref. 42: History Channel (n.d.) Why the US Made Marijuana Illegal
Ref. 43: Charlotte's Web (2020) History of Hemp
Ref. 44: Wikipedia (n.d.) Entheogenic Use of Cannabis
Ref. 45: Herbarium (n.d.) Why Do Some Societies Consider Weed Sacred?
Ref 46: Steven Voser (2020) Sadhus: indian holy men with a unique link to cannabis
Ref. 47: History Channel (n.d.) Rastafarianism
Ref. 48: Isack Cole (2017) The LaGuardia Committee Report – 1944 New York US – The Marihuana Problem In The City Of New York
Ref. 49: Isack Cole (2017) The Marijuana Tax Act Was Signed By Roosevelt 80 Years Ago Starting Federal Marijuana Prohibition In The US
Ref 50: Study.com (n.d.) The Marijuana Tax Act of 1937
Ref. 51: Jamaicans.com (n.d.) Marijuana And Other Rasta Symbols
Ref. 52: Equal Justice Initiative (2018) Black and Hispanic People Are Disproportionately Arrested on Marijuana Charges in New York
Ref. 53: History Channel (n.d.) The Complicated History of Cannabis in the US
Ref. 54: PsyTech Global (n.d.) The Centrality of Set and Setting in Psychedelics
Ref. 55: Don Latin (2020) Bill Wilson, LSD and the Secret Psychedelic History of Alcoholics Anonymous
Ref. 56: Luke Sholl (2020) A Visionary Romance: Steve Jobs and LSD
Ref. 57: Michael Pollan (2022) How to Change Your Mind: LSD, Netflix Documentary
Ref. 58: PHILLIP SMITH (2017) 3 famous philosophers who took psychedelics and pronounced it mind-changing
Ref. 59: Ronit Molko (2022) Psychedelics As Treatment Options For Mental Health, Forbes
Ref. 60: Carla Cantor (2021) Psilocybin Found to Rapidly Improve Depressive Symptoms in Clinical Trial, Columbia University
Ref. 61: Revitalizing Infusion Therapies (2020) Why We Strive for Ego Death With Psychedelics

Ref. 62: Frontiers (2022) Psychedelic Mushrooms in the USA: Knowledge, Patterns of Use, and Association With Health Outcomes
Ref. 63: Donick Cary (2020) Have a Good Trip: Adventures in Psychedelics, Netflix Documentary
Ref. 64: R. Doblin (1998) Dr. Leary's Concord Prison Experiment: a 34-year follow-up study
Ref. 65: Wikipedia (n.d.) Harvard Psilocybin Project
Ref. 66: The Yucatan Times (2022) María Sabina: Saint Mother of the Sacred Mushrooms
Ref. 67: F J Carod-Artal (2015) Hallucinogenic drugs in pre-Columbian Mesoamerican cultures
Ref. 68: Wikipedia (n.d.) Gordon Wasson
Ref. 69: The Oaxaca Post (2022) SOME HISTORICAL FIGURES WHO VISITED OAXACAN MARÍA SABINA, THE GREAT MEXICAN SHAMAN
Ref. 70: Cleveland Clinic (2022) Serotonin
Ref. 71: ANNAMARYA SCACCIA (2017) What Psychedelics Really Do to Your Brain, Rolling Stone
Ref. 72: Northwestern Medicine (n.d.) 7 Reasons to Listen to Your Gut
Ref. 73: Kendra Cherry, MSEd (2022) What Is Neuroplasticity?
Ref. 74: Alcohol and Drug Foundation (2023) Ayahuasca
Ref. 75: Wesley Thoricatha (2015) The Amazonian Caretakers of Ayahuasca: The Shipibo Tribe
Ref. 76: Wikipedia (n.d.) Shamanism
Ref. 77: Wikipedia (n.d.) History of lysergic acid diethylamide
Ref. 78: New Scientist (n.d.) LSD
Ref. 79: Barbara Brody (2022) How to Find and Use Fentanyl Test Strips
Ref. 80: Drugs.com (n.d.) MDMA
Ref. 81: Kirkpatrick, M., Lee, R., Wardle, M., Jacob, S., & de Wit, H. (2014) Ecstasy and Oxytocin
Ref. 82: Drug Policy Alliance (2015) What are the most common adulterants in what's sold as "molly" or "ecstasy" (in other words, what chemicals is it commonly cut with)?
Ref. 83: Will Stone (2019) MDMA, Or Ecstasy, Shows Promise As A PTSD Treatment, NPR
Ref. 84: Wikipedia (n.d.) Mescaline
Ref. 85: Alex Gibbons (n.d.) Psychoactive Cacti - The Psychedelic Effects of Mescaline in Peyote, San Pedro & Peruvian Torch
Ref. 86: Wikipedia (n.d.) *PiHKAL*
Ref. 87: Brandon Ambrosino (2017) The Invention of 'Heterosexuality,' BBC

Ref. 88: National Park Service (2016) Sexual and Gender Diversity in Native America and the Pacific Islands
Ref. 89: CORY COLLINS (2019) Is Queer OK to Say? Here's Why We Use It
Ref. 90: History Channel (n.d.) Stonewall Riots
Ref. 91: Sexuality Education Resource Center (n.d.) Gender Identity
Ref. 92: Ben Jacobs (2015) 'Love is love': Obama lauds gay marriage activists in hailing 'a victory for America'
Ref. 93: Korin Miller (2021) 18 Types of Sexuality To Know for Greater Understanding About Yourself and Others
Ref. 94: History Channel (n.d.) Gay Rights
Ref. 95: Wikipedia (n.d.) Sex change
Ref. 96: Wikipedia (n.d.) Homosexual behavior in animals
Ref. 97: Siobhan Donegan (n.d.) Transgenderism in Ancient Cultures
Ref. 98: Cincinnati Public Library (2020) Queer Poetry Spotlight Series: Audre Lorde & Adrienne Rich
Ref. 99: Wikipedia (n.d.) George Michael
Ref. 100: Rainer Maria Rilke (1929) Letters to a Young Poet
Ref. 101: Katie Stone (2021) A Beginner's Guide To San Pedro
Ref. 102: Sy Safransky (1990) Sunbeams: A Book of Quotations" quote by Rainer Maria Rilke
Ref. 103: Iyanla Van Zant (1998) One Day My Soul Just Opened Up: 40 Days And 40 Nights Towards Spiritual Strength And Personal Growth
Ref. 104: bell hooks (1999) All About Love: New Visions
Ref. 105: IBIS World (2023) Wedding Services in the US - Market Size 2005–2029
Ref. 106: Romana King (2022) Nearly half of American couples go into debt to get married — but is it a good idea?, Yahoo Finance
Ref. 107: Wilkinson & Finkbeiner (2022) DIVORCE STATISTICS: OVER 115 STUDIES, FACTS AND RATES FOR 2022
Ref. 108: Zoe Burke (2021) The 31 Things You Should Definitely Discuss Before Marriage
Ref. 109: Karen Danao (n.d.) 75 Broken Family Quotes to Help You Heal and Grow
Ref. 110: Adrian Body (2023) Adrian Body Quotes & Sayings
Ref. 111: Eckhart Tolle (1997) The Power of Now
Ref. 112: U.S. Customs and Border Protection (2019) Did You Know... Marijuana Was Once a Legal Cross-Border Import?: US Customs and Border Protection
Ref. 113: CYDNEY ADAMS (2016) The man behind the marijuana ban for all the wrong reasons: Cydney Adams, CBS News

Ref 114: The Reefer Madness Museum (n.d.) The Reefer Madness Era: What Was the Anslinger's Gore File

Ref. 115: Chris Kolmar (2023) 26 INCREDIBLE US PHARMACEUTICAL STATISTICS [2023]: FACTS, DATA, TRENDS AND MORE

Ref. 116: Centers for Disease Control and Prevention (2021) Drug Overdose Deaths in the U.S. Up 30% in 2020

Ref. 117: Cancer Research UK (2021) Age and cancer

Ref. 118: By Kirsten Nunez (2021) How to Navigate the Cost of Chemotherapy, Healthline

Ref. 119: Noam Levey (2022) She was already battling cancer. Then she had to fight the bill collectors, NPR

Ref: 120: Memorial Sloan Kettering Cancer Center (2023) Gerson Therapy: National Cancer Institute

Ref. 121: Wikipedia (n.d.) Harry J. Anslinger

Ref. 122: News Beat (2017) Racism, Weed & Jazz: The True Origins of the War on Drugs, Medium

Ref. 123: Surviving Mexico (2021) Natural Healing — Peyote

Ref. 124: Stephen Woodman (2018) Peyote: 10 Incredible Health Benefits of Mexico's Psychedelic Plant

Ref. 125: PSYCHEDELIC MEDICINE PODCAST WITH DR. LYNN MARIE MORSKI (n.d.) Microdosing Q&A with James Fadiman

Ref. 126: Neel Burton M.D. (2015) When Homosexuality Stopped Being a Mental Disorder, Psychology Today

Ref. 127: ACLU (2023) Mapping Attacks on LGBTQ Rights in U.S. State Legislatures

Ref. 128: Allison Abrams, LCSW-R (2023) Navigating the 4 Stages of a Relationship

Ref. 129: Joe Cambray (n.d.) Synchronicity: An Acausal Connecting Principle, INTERNATIONAL ASSOCIATION FOR ANALYTICAL PSYCHOLOGY

Ref. 130: Paulo Friere (1968) Pedagogy of the Oppressed

Ref. 131: Uvanney Maylor (2012) Key Pedagogic Thinkers: Paulo Friere, University of Bedfordshire Journal Of Pedagogic Development, Volume 2 Issue 3 November 2012

Ref. 132: The Hunger Project (2021) Know Your World

Ref. 133: Minimalist Quotes (2020) Fidel Castro

Ref. 134: Che Guevara Quotes (n.d.)

Ref. 135: Garrett Parker (2023) 5 Huge Companies Known For Implementing Horrific Working Conditions, Money Inc

Ref. 136: *Living Buddhism (*April 2023) 40 Years of Ikeda Sensei's Peace Proposals

Ref. 137: Martin Rowinski (2022) How Small Businesses Drive The American Economy, Forbes
Ref. 138: Grace Beard (2018) How Countries Take a Break Around the World
Ref. 139: *THE LEARNING CURVE (JANUARY 24, 2023)* The world must learn from "karoshi," Japan's overwork epidemic — before it's too late, Big Think
Ref. 140: Wikipedia (n.d.) Hurricane Katrina
Ref. 141: Euronews Travel (2023) Italy travel: Everything you need to know as cleanup begins after 'apocalyptic' floods
Ref. 142: FloodList (n.d.)
Ref. 143: Douglas Fox (July 1, 2012) Scientists Trek to Collapsing Glaciers to Assess Antarctica's Meltdown and Sea-Level Rise, Scientific American
Ref. 144: Ashley Thomson (2020) Biodiversity and the Amazon Rainforest, Greenpeace
Ref. 145: ClientEarth Communications (2021) What is biodiversity and why is it important?
Ref. 146: CDC Museum COVID-19 Timeline (n.d.)
Ref. 147: Govind Bhutada (2023) Visualizing the Scale of Global Fossil Fuel Production, Visual Capitalist
Ref. 148/150: Reuters (2023) Oil and gas industry earned $4 trillion last year, says IEA chief - Reuters
Ref. 149: Greenpeace (n.d.) Forest Destruction
Ref. 151: ANDRIY BLOKHIN (2023) The 5 Countries That Produce the Most Carbon Dioxide (CO2)
Ref. 152: UN Environment Program (n.d.) Indigenous peoples and the nature they protect
Ref. 153: Conciliation Resources (November 2022) The Indigenous communities facing the climate crisis in the Philippines
Ref. 154: UN Department of Economic and Social Affairs Indigenous Peoples (2007) Climate Change
Ref. 155: Paul Brian (2021) The 15 most important thinkers in permaculture
Ref. 156: LaPorsche Thomas (2021) The story behind Martin Luther King Jr.'s first major boycott
Ref. 157: Juliana McDonald (2023) Curbing America's Trash Production: Statistics and Solutions
Ref. 157: UN Environment Program (n.d.) Plastic Pollution
Ref. 158: ANNIE GREENBERG (2022) Plastic Free July: How 20 countries are taking action - Sustainable Ocean Alliance

Ref. 159: National Geographic (n.d.) Great Pacific Garbage Patch
Ref. 160: Jeff Turrentine (2022) What Are the Solutions to Climate Change? NRDC
Ref. 161: Environmental and Energy Study Institute (2021) Fossil Fuels
Ref. 162: United Nations (n.d.) Climate Action
Ref. 163: United Nations (n.d.) Renewable energy – powering a safer future
Ref. 164: David Spratt (2023) Faster than forecast, climate impacts trigger tipping points in the Earth system, Bulletin on the Atomic Sciences
Ref. 165: Climate Council (n.d.) 11 COUNTRIES LEADING THE CHARGE ON RENEWABLE ENERGY
Ref. 166: IEA (26 April 2023) Demand for electric cars is booming, with sales expected to leap 35% this year after a record-breaking 2022
Ref. 167: Nina Lakhani (2022) US transition to electric vehicles would save over 100,000 lives by 2050, The Guardian
Ref. 168: Jane Marsh (2022) Will Renewables Make Public Transportation More Affordable? Renewable Energy Magazine
Ref. 169: Wikipedia (n.d.) Slow movement (culture)
Ref. 170: Liz Kimbrough (18 October 2022) Beef is still coming from protected areas in the Amazon, study shows, Mongabay
Ref. 171: Copper Utensils Online Wholesale & Manufacturers (2017) Why Our Ancestors Preferred Storing Water in copper utensils, Medium
Ref. 172: Dr. Nikita Toshi (2023) 15 Benefits Of Drinking Water From Copper Bottle Vessels, PharmEasy
Ref. 173: Katie DeMuro (July 11, 2013) The Many Benefits of Community Gardens
Ref. 174: Wikipedia (n.d.) 23 September 2019: United Nations Climate Action Summit – "How dare you!" - Greta Thurnberg
Ref. 175: MICHAEL SVOBODA (FEBRUARY 21, 2023) Book review: Greta Thunberg tells it like it is in "The Climate Book," Yale Climate Connections
Ref. 176: Sarah Lawless (September 16, 2022) Mayan Civilizations: Sustainability Pioneers
Ref. 177: Dan Buettner (n.d.) Blue Zones
Ref. 178: CORI BROSNAHAN (2020) Despite Recycling Success, S.F.'s Zero Waste Goal Remains Elusive, SF Public Press
Ref. 179: Clarisa Diaz (April 19, 2023) Where marijuana is legal in the US in 2023
Ref. 180: Deena Zaru (2022) Timeline of Brittney Griner's detention in Russia as US secures her release, ABC News

Ref. 181: Indigenous Futures (2021) The Future is a territory to defend, Cool Hunter MX
Ref. 182: Northwestern Medicine (2023) 7 Reasons to Listen to Your Gut
Ref. 183: Bella All Natural (2021) CHLOROPHYLL, CHLORELLA, AND SPIRULINA: WHAT'S THE DIFFERENCE?
Ref. 184: Jonathan Guyer (2022) Why Brittney Griner was released now, VOX
Ref. 185: NATALIE OGANESYAN (February 7, 2020) To Be Blunt: Cannabis is an integral part of jazz history in America
Ref. 186: Alexander Tabibi, MD (2021) Top 5 Jazz Musicians Who Used Weed
Ref. 187: Doobie Nights (2020) EVOLUTION OF CANNABIS THROUGH THE DECADES
Ref. 188: Donna Mazzola, Pharmd (n.d.) The Magical Healing Power of Plants
Ref. 189: "Fresh Air" with Maureen Corrigan ('2017) A Really Good Day' Recaps A Month-Long Adventure Of Microdosing LSD: NPR
Ref. 190: ICEERS (n.d.) Bufo Toad (Incilius alvarius):
Ref. 191: Adrienne Santos-Longhurst (2021) DMT and the Pineal Gland: Separating Fact from Fiction
Ref. 192: Annabelle Bartz (2021) Seahorses and gender roles in the natural world
Ref. 193: BBC (2017) Straight women have fewest orgasms
Ref. 194: Franny White (2022) Pleasure-producing human clitoris has more than 10,000 nerve fibers, OHSU
Ref. 195: Deccan Chronicle (2017) Just 1 out of 10 women able to orgasm during one night stands: study
Ref. 196: Lyss Welding (2022) Federal vs. Private Student Loan Debt Over Time, Best Colleges

Made in the USA
Las Vegas, NV
25 February 2024

85958873R00125